BETWEEN GOOD AND EVIL

ALSO BY MELLISSA FUNG

Under an Afghan Sky: A Memoir of Captivity

BETWEEN GOOD AND EVIL

The Stolen Girls of Boko Haram

MELLISSA FUNG

HarperCollins Publishers Ltd

Published by HarperCollins Publishers Ltd

First edition

HarperCollins books may be purchased for educational, business
or sales promotional use through our Special Markets Department.

HarperCollins Publishers Ltd
Bay Adelaide Centre, East Tower
22 Adelaide Street West, 41st Floor
Toronto, Ontario, Canada
M5H 4E3

www.harpercollins.ca

All interior photographs courtesy of the author.
Map by Mary Rostad.

Library and Archives Canada Cataloguing in Publication

Title: Between good and evil : the stolen girls of Boko Haram / Mellissa Fung.
Names: Fung, Mellissa, author. | Description: Includes bibliographical references.
Identifiers: Canadiana (print) 20220442592 | Canadiana (ebook) 2022044367X
ISBN 9781443456081 (hardcover) | ISBN 9781443456098 (EPUB)
Subjects: LCSH: Schoolgirls—Nigeria—Biography. | LCSH: Women—Nigeria—Biography.
LCSH: Kidnapping victims—Nigeria—Biography. | LCSH: Schoolgirls—Crimes against—
Nigeria. | LCSH: Schoolgirls—Violence against—Nigeria. | LCSH: Schoolgirls—Abuse of—
Nigeria. | LCSH: Boko Haram. | LCSH: Terrorism—Nigeria. | LCSH: Abduction—Nigeria.
LCGFT: Biographies. | Classification: LCC HV6433.N62 B655 2023
DDC 362.88/93170925309669—dc23

Printed and bound in the United States of America
23 24 25 26 27 LBC 5 4 3 2 1

FOR PAUL,
WHO MAKES ME BELIEVE THAT ANYTHING IS POSSIBLE

That night, we were in the forest. I didn't know how long we would be there. Where was my family? My mother, my father, my sisters, my brothers? Would I ever see them again?

—ASMA'U, taken aged twelve

CONTENTS

AUTHOR'S NOTE

THIS STORY BELONGS to the brave and beautiful survivors of Boko Haram who trusted me to give voice to their struggles. I have chosen to focus on their narratives rather than trace the rise of Boko Haram and examine the Nigerian government's efforts to bring the long insurgency to an end. There are many more learned writers who have produced works about that history, and I relied on their expertise here to construct the backdrop to the trauma the girls endured. Alexander Thurston's definitive account of the terror group's rise, *Boko Haram: The History of an African Jihadist Movement*, was the most thorough and meticulously researched account of the group's history I came across. For the translations of speeches by the group's founder, Muhammad Yusuf, I turned to *The Boko Haram Reader: From Nigerian Preachers to the Islamic State*, edited by Abdulbasit Kassim and Michael Nwankpa. I have also relied on many news accounts of individual battles and attacks, from sources including the *Guardian*, Al Jazeera, the BBC, the *New York Times*, the *Daily*

Trust (Nigeria), and numerous academic papers to help paint a picture of events that took place years ago.

Northeastern Nigeria and especially the regions controlled by Boko Haram are not easily accessible places to study, so I am deeply indebted to the work of many journalists, researchers, and academics. Their tireless efforts have greatly informed this book.

BETWEEN GOOD AND EVIL

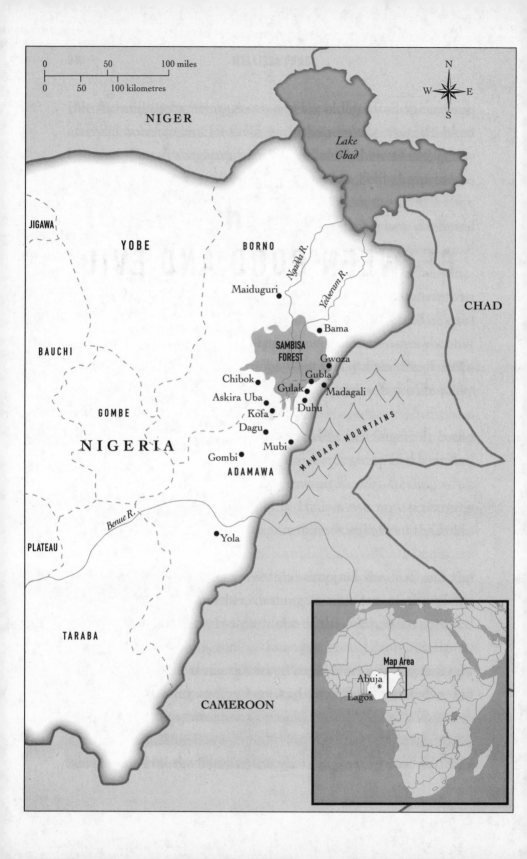

THE GIRLS IN THE FOREST

IT WAS A CLEAR NIGHT, the night of April 14, 2014. A gang of armed men broke into a girls' boarding school in the town of Chibok, in northeastern Nigeria, intent on stealing an engine of some sort. There may have been construction going on at the school. There have been many accounts of what these men were looking for and what actually happened that night, but no one disputes that by the next morning, 276 girls were missing. They had already spent their first night in the Sambisa forest—their first night in captivity. I didn't know much about the Sambisa then, but over time, I would come to understand the forest as a dark, ungovernable expanse that even government forces found difficult to penetrate, the perfect sanctuary to grow a terrorist movement. That movement was called Boko Haram—which translates roughly to "Western education is forbidden"—and this was one of its most brazen attacks.

When I woke up to the news thousands of miles away in Washington, DC, where I was living at the time, my stomach began to cramp and a cold tremble of foreboding, one I knew well, coursed through my body as I scanned the headlines on Twitter. "Fears Captive Girls Will Be Used as Sex Slaves," read one. "Nigerian Government Says Military Operation Underway to Search for Kidnapped Girls," said another. As I read, a familiarity—a muscle memory of trauma—twitched in my head and tightened in my chest as I imagined the girls' fears, their confusion, as they spent their first night as captives.

The word "kidnap" has been a trigger for me since late 2008, when I was taken at gunpoint by a similar band of armed men. Except that was in Afghanistan, not Nigeria. A hole in the ground in Wardak Province, not the Sambisa forest in Borno State. Men sympathetic to the Taliban, not Boko Haram. But once a hostage, you become a hostage to your memories, and certain words become triggers that have you staring down the dark barrel into a place you have no desire to return to and no choice but to revisit. It is the dread that lurks in your subconscious, ready to pounce when you least expect it.

Every time I hear of a taking, I think of the taken. Journalists. Aid workers. Contractors. Those violently removed from the world they know, the freedoms they're accustomed to, the ordinariness of daily life. Suddenly, their world shrinks to the confines of their captivity. Whether that's a forest or a small room or a hole in the ground, the loss of the ordinary and the known is frightening. You wrestle with your mortality every day, as if death is very close by: around the corner, inside your head, in your captors' hands. In captivity, you constantly dance with death. Some days, that dance is like a waltz, tiptoeing around the possibility; other times, it's more like a dare, where you almost will your captors to shoot you, just to end the misery.

You become acutely aware of the fragility of life, and of the fact that you often have no control over when your life might end. Living every day with the possibility of dying at any moment brings many things into sharp focus, and yet it makes others very blurry.

When you're taken, you're no longer in control of yourself. The loss of freedom, the uncertainty of the outcome. The guns. The guns! Pointed at you. And if you're a woman—the men. The men. Who threaten not just because of their gender, their size, their weapons, but also because they expose your vulnerability, no matter how strong you believe yourself to be.

News of the Chibok kidnapping reopened the invisible scars I have mostly tried to ignore in the years since my own kidnapping. I scratched at them by devouring all the news I could find. How was this possible? Where did the girls go? Who was trying to save them? Michelle Obama tweeted "#BringBackOurGirls," and with that one hashtag, the international community was engaged. Everyone seemed to be invested in the fate of these girls. Now "our" girls. Whose girls?

That answer should be obvious. Every hostage has a family. And what that family endures is unfathomable. I still have not been able to talk to my family about the ordeal they went through those four weeks in the fall of 2008, when I was in the hole. I know vaguely from my sister that my dad almost ran over a pedestrian after leaving a meeting where the hostage-negotiating team told my family I might already be dead.

I knew the girls' families were no doubt feeling the same sense of panic, the same disbelief that their daughters could simply vanish, be disappeared overnight, just like that. Families left to wonder, Is she still alive? And if she is, where is she being kept? What horrors is she having to endure? How can we sleep not knowing where she is? How can we wake up not knowing if she will? How can we walk knowing she is confined? Are they treating her with some dignity? How could they not?

But I knew better what the girls themselves were thinking. Because I had thought the same things from the second I resigned myself to captivity. With that resignation comes many other feelings. Guilt, for putting your parents through the trauma of not knowing. Distress, at the thought of how they may or may not be coping. Fear, of how it all might end.

The thought of being held hostage in a forest seemed singularly terrifying. But as I read and learned more about Boko Haram, I realized that this was far from an isolated incident. The Chibok girls were just a small number of the hostages these men had taken into the forest. The reality was that thousands of girls—victims of the everyday kidnappings that had been taking place for years before Chibok—were missing. No one even knew the exact number. The crisis was compounded by the fact that there were potentially hundreds, if not thousands, of girls who had escaped but were now shunned by their families and their communities for being "wives and mothers" of Boko Haram. Innocent girls caught through no fault of their own in a never-ending spiral of terror and pain.

The Sambisa forest was not always a place of horror. Once known as the Sambisa game reserve, it was a vast stretch of lush savannah home to elephants, leopards, hyenas, baboons, and sixty-two different species of birds.[1] Nigeria's British colonizers had set the Sambisa aside as a conservation area in 1958, two years before they left the country to chart its own destiny. Fed by two rivers, the Ngadda and the Yedseram, the reserve boasted stunning natural beauty and towering baobab, rubber, and date palm trees. Until the 1970s, it was a destination for international tourists in search of a unique safari experience.

But when the British left, the game reserve quickly fell victim to neglect and corruption by park management. Funds were misused, budgets mishandled. Colonel Ibrahim Babangida, then the military governor of Borno State and later the president of Nigeria, proposed establishing military-style training camps in the Sambisa and using the national guard to patrol the area.[2] Babangida's critics accused him of organizing a private army to hold on to power, and the public outcry prevented these ideas from becoming reality. Instead, poachers and hunters moved in, and over the years, the animals slowly disappeared.

And then Sambisa became a conveniently perfect place for Boko Haram militants to hide out. But they did more than that—they converted the bases that had been set up for the failed national guard initiative into their headquarters. This would be their command centre, the place where they plotted their reign of terror. The place where they kept the girls they took hostage.

The more I thought about it, the more horrific the whole situation seemed. No one even knows how many girls have been lost to the Sambisa. In 2019, after a decade of conflict, the International Committee of the Red Cross estimated that throughout Nigeria, more than twenty-two thousand people were missing, many of them women and children. How could there be so many missing girls the world doesn't know about? Why wasn't this front-page news? Why weren't people more outraged that this had been allowed to happen, largely with impunity? And the girls who'd managed to escape or were rescued—how were they coping with the aftermath of trauma? Were they back in school? Did they have access to therapists and counsellors? Who was supporting them?

I was fully aware that my own experience as a captive stoked my outrage, but as a journalist, I was astounded that there had been so little coverage of the conflict in Nigeria until the Chibok kidnappings. I was also aware that in any conflict, women and girls suffer the most; they bear the biggest burden. Violence against women is often downplayed in war, but rape is one of history's oldest weapons. This is a space writers much more eloquent than I am have explored in depth, but as a survivor, I have a special interest in how people recover from the trauma of being taken. After my captors had released me in a deal with the Afghan government, I was fortunate enough to work with a wonderful therapist who helped me navigate my post-traumatic stress and made me understand that my sometimes debilitating rage and my many recurring nightmares were actually manifestations of that trauma. Years later, I still suffer the occasional setback—the nightmares return at certain times of the year—but I know what my triggers are, and I have come to appreciate my own strengths and shortcomings when dealing with stress and memories.

I know what a luxury it is to have the support I had—the best trauma therapists in Canada, the help of friends and family. But I also have an idea of the stigma that being a captive can carry. I returned to my work in the newsroom, but I found out quickly that my status had changed. I wasn't shunned—on the contrary, people went out of their way to be kind and caring—but I was passed over for assignments that might involve risk. I realized I would not be going into conflict zones anymore. That was hard for me; I wanted to carry on doing the kind of journalism I felt was important—stories about women and girls affected by war. My frustration at being unable to return to Afghanistan and tell the stories I wanted to boiled over. I was told that many considered me "difficult," and as I look back now, I know I was, because I did not want to be defined by what had happened to me. My unhappiness reached a point where I had to leave the job I loved to preserve my own sanity, but I harboured a resentment that simmered for years afterward. My mental health suffered in ways I still find hard to describe, and anger became my crutch.

So when I found out that the young women who had escaped Boko Haram's grasp were now being shunned by their communities—and even their own families—I felt my rage rising again on their behalf. I needed to witness this myself; I needed to know how these girls were dealing with their trauma, their ostracism, their suffering in an inhospitable region beset by violence. I wanted to learn from their experiences. I was curious to see if trauma could transcend borders and language barriers when women come together to share their stories.

And so began a years-long journey to uncover some of Nigeria's hidden secrets. Between 2016 and 2020, I made several trips to the country, some alone and some with a film crew in tow, to meet and get to know many extraordinary young women who found the fortitude to share their stories with me. This book would not exist without Kabir Anwar, the local journalist who became my guide and my connection to the girls. Through him and his friend Ibrahim, who was a cousin to one of the girls, named Gambo, I was introduced to Asma'u, another cousin, and their friend Zara.* They pulled back the curtain on their struggle to rebuild lives that had been torn apart by Boko Haram. And along the way, I met other incredible women trying to do their part to bring healing, justice, and hope to these girls and other former captives. When I could, I tried to connect them, even though that meant stepping over the traditional boundaries of journalism. My own experience told me I had to try.

I was completely honest with all the girls about what motivated me to tell their stories. As a journalist, it is often too easy to exploit other people's trauma. So I opened up to them about my own. Sharing our experiences helped them see that they were not alone. They were amazed that someone like me— so different from them in every other way—could have been through an ordeal so similar to theirs. That was the starting point for this conversation, which continues to this day and will carry on past this book.

This is their story—their grief, their pain, their lives. I've tried my best to reconstruct the girls' struggles from the hundreds of hours of interviews I conducted over more than four years. In 2021, I had planned yet another trip—to reconfirm their stories—but it had to be scrapped due to Covid, so Kabir painstakingly did that work for me. Some expressions in Hausa don't necessarily translate into English with the same resonance,

---

* I have changed the names of some of the girls who feature less prominently in this story. There were many girls and women named Aisha (it's a very popular name in Nigeria), and I feared it would be too hard to keep their stories distinct. For clarity, I have given them unique names.

but I've done the best I can to relay events with the same emotion and meaning. And sometimes memories—theirs and mine—are hazy, especially when they involve trauma. Even in the few years I have known the girls, time has eroded some memories and sharpened others, so I have done the same in reconstructing their experiences, while staying as true as I can to each story as a whole. I may have conflated some details from the many retellings, but I've tried to the best of my ability to hew as closely as I can to their recollections. I was also very aware of not wanting to put the girls through the pain of reliving their trauma over and over again. These accounts have come out slowly and sporadically—some in interviews with me, and others in videotaped conversations among themselves or talks with other people, such as friends, family members, and some trauma counsellors I introduced them to. I have also tried to put myself into their shoes, gathering their thoughts and memories and translating them into what I hope is a narrative that takes the reader into their collective nightmare, their ongoing struggle to rewrite their story, and their search for the kind of peace that comes from defining themselves not as victims but as survivors.

PROLOGUE
MAMA BOKO HARAM

MAMA BOKO HARAM was in her office in Maiduguri, the capital of Borno State, on the phone. She spent a lot of time on the phone these days. The room was cramped; an oversized desk took up much of the space, but an air conditioner mounted above the window blew down cool air. Still, she fanned herself with an envelope as she cradled the receiver between her ear and her shoulder. Her mind was starting to drift from the conversation when her cellphone rang. She looked at the number on the display and blurted into the receiver, "I'll call you back later." With that, she hung up the landline and picked up her cell, launching into a negotiation with the person on the other end about where and when to meet. It seemed urgent.

"Tell Nneka we're going there. Yes, I know the way. If I go to Jasko's supply station . . . where's the station? Yes! And then I turn left or right? Okay, we will be there."

She motioned for the program manager of her foundation, a tall older man dressed in a light-coloured long robe and dark pants, the traditional outfit of the Yoruba. He smiled and bent over her desk, ready to take direction. He had been doing so for a while now.

She whispered a few words into his ear. He nodded and walked out of the room. The rendezvous was set. It was a little progress at a time when there hadn't been much. She then picked up her office phone and dialled her daughter, Ummi, whom she'd cut off earlier when the cell call came in.

She hadn't meant to hang up so abruptly, but there was a lot on her mind. She was in deep negotiations with a senior commander of Boko Haram to bring out some of the Chibok girls. No one—not even the government—knew how many girls were still in this man's custody, but she had an opportunity to negotiate their freedom. She couldn't let anyone know, however. Her greatest fear was that the security forces would arrest or even kill him if they discovered her plan. They had done that before. One time, she convinced about a dozen fighters to surrender, and as soon as they came out of the forest, government forces swooped in and killed them all. Mama was livid. It made her uneasy and unsure about proceeding with what already seemed like an impossible mission. But she knew she had to try. Many of her "sons" were tired of the fighting, tired of living rough in the forest. They were ready to come out and surrender. They just needed Mama to help them make the transition back to civilian life, to get them out from under the tight grip and outsized influence of a man they both respected and feared. Their leader, Abubakar Shekau.

How did an Igbo woman from the south come to be known as Mama to the Kanuri boys of the north? It's a story that sometimes surprises Mama herself. And it's one she never tires of telling, mainly because she wants people—particularly outsiders and foreigners—to understand that the feared terrorists they know as Boko Haram were once young boys wandering the streets of Maiduguri, lost and hungry.

Mama was raised a devout Christian, a Catholic who grew up studying the Bible in the Igbo south. But her path took an unexpected turn when she decided to go to university in Maiduguri in the late 1980s. It was there that she met Gana Alkali Wakil, a Muslim from the Kanuri tribe. She likes to think that there are no coincidences in life, and that she was destined to meet Gana because she was needed in this part of the country. There was never any question that she would convert to Islam. In Kanuri culture, the woman always has to follow the man. But Mama did not see her conversion as a gender issue. After all, it was her *choice*—she did not want to marry into a traditional Kanuri family and not respect the culture. So she happily donned the full hijab, covering her beautiful face, which had drawn much attention at university—not just from Gana but from other young students and even a few professors. She was a willing and true convert, trading in the Bible for the Qur'an, which she studied with a curious mind and an open heart. She looked at the world through the opening in her hijab, her eyes the only window into her mind, and she revealed very little through that small slit. Everything was held inside. Aisha Wakil became her Muslim name, the one she took after marriage. Her Christian name was discarded with her past and is known only to her and those who knew her in her previous life. It is as if the woman she was before she married and converted had never existed, and in her place stood a devout Muslim wife and mother—not just to her own children but eventually to a generation of boys who needed a mother figure to fill a gap in their lives.

Maiduguri in the early 1990s was a dust bowl of a city gradually transforming because of urban sprawl. One of the first things Mama noticed when she arrived was that the infrastructure was unable to keep up with the growth. And compared to cities in the richer south, it was far from a metropolis. She saw boys wandering the streets in packs, not quite threatening but somehow quietly aggressive in a way that made her wonder what was really happening in the seams of this rambling city.

Mama believed that poverty and the almajiri school system were to blame for the many social problems she saw. Under the almajiri system, young boys from poor families were placed in Islamic schools where the only subject taught was the Qur'an. Why, she wondered, was it good policy to teach boys religion without also teaching them theology, Arabic, other subjects and skills that they could use more practically? But poverty forces poor choices on parents who have neither resources nor energy to fight for better. The children were now defined by the only schooling they had—even the word "almajiri" came to mean street boys, urchins. To Mama, they might as well have been called the children society had failed.

After graduation, she and Gana married and she moved into his family's compound. Both were trained as barristers. His career took off and he worked his way up, becoming a respected judge in Maiduguri. Mama also threw herself into work, mediating disputes in the community and establishing a reputation as a trustworthy source of advice.

Looking back, she realized that by opening her doors to the community, she—an outsider—was giving the young men she had seen wandering the streets a place of shelter and nourishment. She showed them that someone cared. She could provide what they were not getting from their parents, from their schools, from the government. At first, the boys who came to her were young—six, seven, eight years old. She would help with their circumcisions, holding their hands as they were being cut and then pouring hot water to clean the incision. They started calling her Mama because that's how they saw her: a mother figure who fed them when they were hungry and comforted them when they were hurting. (She has been known as Mama for so long now that she sometimes forgets to answer to her given name, Aisha.) In time, even their parents started coming to her. On weekends, she would cook enough to feed the neighbourhood and send everyone home with food for the following day. She would buy clothes for the boys if she saw that they were running around with rips in their pants or holes in their shirts. Even when she had children of her own, she continued to concern herself with the welfare of the almajiri boys, whom she'd come to see as her sons. Saturdays were spent in her large garden, drinking tea and tending to her plants. She taught the boys to be great stewards of nature, and they would joke and laugh as they watered her flowers and trimmed her trees. She would cook them a big dinner and send them home, well fed and happy.

But as the boys got older, she noticed that some stopped coming around. One of her favourites, a boy she called Abdul, disappeared for several months, and when he finally returned, his demeanour had completely changed. Instead of checking on her plants after all this time away, he sat in a corner of her garden, his head buried in the Qur'an.

"Abdul, tell me what you are reading," she asked.

But he didn't respond. He looked up at her and then turned back to the verse he was meditating on.

She cajoled him, teasing and laughing, but his expression was blank. She suddenly realized she couldn't reach him, this boy she had known for half his life. This boy who had once laughed and played and wrapped his arms around her after a weekend meal— "Thank you, Mama. I love you." This boy she had fed and clothed and *loved*. He had been somewhere. Somewhere so far from her that she could not even imagine. Now he was silent and brooding. And an uneasiness took root in her heart.

She asked the others, "What is wrong with him?"

"Mama, he went away for training, but now he is back."

"Training? What kind of training?"

Silence. But deep down, Mama knew. There was something happening with the boys, and she felt powerless to stop it. She felt unsettled by it.

Ultimately, Abdul came to her.

"Mama, I know you are asking where I went. I will tell you that I went for training."

"Training for what?" Mama was trying to sound naive, but she braced herself for the answer.

"I was learning how to shoot, Mama!"

"Shoot? That's wonderful. You know that antelope meat is delicious on a fire."

"No, Mama, I was learning how to shoot humans."

"What?"

"Shooting people, Mama."

Mama laughed. She laughed so hard that she was starting to feel cramps in both her sides. Her whole body shook because she could not imagine that this lovely boy could ever kill an antelope, let alone a human. Looking back on that conversation years later, she knew that it was nervous laughter, and that she wanted Abdul to see the folly in his words. When she finally stopped laughing, she noticed he was looking down at her feet.

"Come on, Abdul. Be serious."

"Mama, I'm serious. You are laughing at me, but I am not making a joke."

"Tell me, who is teaching you this?" Mama gave one last attempt at a laugh.

"Muhammad," he said, referring to one of the boys she knew. "But he won't talk to you anymore. He is not one of your sons anymore."

"He won't talk to me?"

"Mama, he is buying guns for us."

"Guns?"

"We bought guns. AK-47s. Do you know what those are? AK-47s?"

"AK-47? What is that?"

"It's a gun. A big gun." Abdul sounded impatient with her.

What was he doing, talking about guns and murder?

"Tell Muhammad to come to me. I want to talk to him, ask him what he's teaching you."

"We are all just at the mosque for an extension of our Qur'anic studies. Why are you so worried about it?"

"I don't like this talk about killing. Who are you trying to kill?"

"Mama, you don't understand." And then he got up and walked away from her, taking his holy book and settling under a tree. He didn't even look up when she brought his tea to him.

She was so troubled by that conversation that she went to her husband the next day.

"Bring me Muhammad Yusuf," she said. "I want to talk to him."

Even though Gana was a judge, he wasn't sure he could make this young preacher come to her. It was clear that Yusuf didn't do anything he didn't want to do.

"Why?" he asked her. "For what? This guy has been creating all kinds of controversy in town. What point are you trying to make?"

"Just get him to come to me. He came here as a young boy, so why wouldn't he come now? I want to talk to him."

"He's been denigrating the government, saying terrible things. The government is going to move against him." Her husband had heard talk among government officials that the military had had just about enough of this rebel movement in the north.

"That's why I want to talk to him."

A few days later, Muhammad Yusuf stood in her doorway, his smile wide and his eyes dancing. He was a slight young man who radiated a boyish charm.

"*Sannu*, Mama."

"Yusuf, what are you doing? You're insulting the government and your elders. Why?"

"Mama, what they are doing is not good. They're not doing the will of Allah. They have gotten power and now are greedy and stealing from poor people like us. They are just taking everything for themselves, and they do not care about us."

"That is for Allah to decide, not us. We must follow his teachings. And they are in government because Allah has put them there, so if you insult them, you are disrespecting Allah."

Yusuf looked her in the eye. He stared intently through the gleam of her glasses into that small opening in the black cloth that covered her face.

"Mama, I do not want to argue with you. I respect you too much. But know that there are bad actors in the government. They do not care about us."

"So what are you going to do about it?"

"We're going to go to war. We'll wage war on inequality and our living conditions. Do you see how dirty our water is? What kind of government would allow us to drink poisons? Who is going to look after us if we do not stand up for ourselves? We are fighting for everyone!"

Mama studied his face closely. She didn't quite know what she was looking for, but she could not detect any real malice. It seemed to her he had convictions—rooted in the Qur'an, perhaps—but was looking for justice in his own way.

"Killing is not going to solve anything, Yusuf. Let me talk to the government."

"Mama, this is not for you to worry about. I'm going now."

"Let me try."

He looked directly into her eyes and gave a slight nod. And then he was gone.

The next day, Mama got on the phone and tried to raise politicians representing Maiduguri to warn them of the insurrection she feared was inevitable. She was hopeful that these politicians might reach out and listen to the concerns of young men in the north and at least meet them where they stood. But it was Ramadan, and that was enough of an excuse for them to put her off.

After a few days, Yusuf appeared at her door again.

"Did you talk to them, Mama?"

"It's Ramadan. Give me a few more days. They are all busy. Give me a bit more time. I can help you fix this. If I don't hear back, I will go to their houses myself. I know where they live. Please just let me try."

Yusuf looked down. "Mama, you're not a politician. Of course they are not taking your calls. We will do this our way. I am alone in this. We are alone in this."

Mama was feeling desperate. "Please, my son, just let me try again."

"It's hopeless. I am alone in this."

Mama called again and again. Ramadan was over now, and it was clear to her that even the politicians she had known in Lagos were not going to take her calls or listen to what she had to say. Yusuf knew this already. He and his followers were getting bolder as they planned their revolution. They walked the streets of Maiduguri brandishing bows and arrows and guns, like a gang that threatened by its very presence. Mama did not like what she was seeing, but she could not raise anyone in power to get them to pay attention.

In a way, she was already too late. Yusuf had started preaching several years earlier at a mosque he'd set up near the railway tracks in a less developed, more deserted part of the city known as the Railway Quarters. This is where her boys were spending more and more of their time. It would eventually become known as the birthplace of Boko Haram.

Yusuf was preaching against everything but sharia. He was angry at everyone. He felt that the government was adopting Western forms of education and culture, which was *haram*, or forbidden, in sharia law. America, he preached, embodied an existential threat to Islam and the Muslim way of life. He used the wars in Iraq and Afghanistan to underscore this point. On several occasions, Mama went to the mosque, called Ibn Taymiyyah, to listen in, to try to understand where Yusuf was coming from. She heard a passionate speaker, a dynamic preacher, and a charismatic leader who was stirring devotion in his followers. Some nodded in agreement as he spoke, while others shouted their approval. Yusuf had them all in his thrall. Where Mama had tempered the disaffections of her sons with love and food and warmth and conversation, Yusuf had ignited them with rhetoric and religion and community and purpose. There was nothing more she could have done to prevent that; she was losing her boys to another boy she had always considered a son. She turned this over and over in her head, losing sleep, questioning herself, wondering how she had failed to see his growing influence among the boys. But she could not have known what was in Yusuf's mind, what had settled into his soul.

One of Yusuf's wives (he had four, or so Mama was told) was the daughter of Baba Fugu, a man Mama considered to be her spiritual father. He was her guide when she'd converted to Islam, and he had read through the Qur'an with her when she was learning the holy book as part of her initiation into the religion. She'd looked to him to answer the questions any Christian might have about Islam. He was generous with his knowledge and wisdom, and through prayer and reconciliation, her Muslim faith had deepened. Baba always made time for her. Even as she opened her gates to the boys, he was a constant touchstone, always there as a guide if she needed, asking the right questions to make her come to an understanding on her own. Some weekends, she would bring her meals to Baba's compound, not far from the railway station, and watch as Yusuf and his followers piled their plates high with rice and stew.

A few years after Yusuf started his mosque, he married Baba's daughter, Amina, and Mama saw this as perhaps another way to get closer to him, to try to understand what he was preaching and how he was influencing her boys. But Yusuf was already beyond her grasp. He had amassed a following that even he did not think possible. The majority were poor almajiri who had grown up around the railroad tracks, uneducated and unemployable, but others had money and influence. One day, Yusuf showed up at Mama's gates in a fancy new car.

"Where did you get that?" She almost didn't want to hear the answer.

"From someone who likes what I'm saying, Mama. I forget his name. He's a big man, a big man from Abuja."

"A big gift from a big man."

Mama knew that Yusuf's growing following was gaining attention in government. How could it not? She watched the crowds grow larger by the week, and she took notice of the fancy cars with tinted windows crowding into the railway area.

Who they were ferrying she couldn't tell, but she knew he was attracting some powerful patrons. The powers that be couldn't ignore him much longer, but for now, they didn't seem to want to engage.

Mama decided to speak with Baba, now Yusuf's father-in-law, and seek counsel, as she always did when she felt there was something beyond her grasp. But by then, even he believed it was too late. He had been watching Yusuf very carefully and had noticed subtle changes Mama didn't see. He told her he had already written a letter to the secretary of the government. But he wasn't optimistic at all. "They have made up their minds already," he whispered quietly to her. "I have told them everything that I know. They are just waiting for his next move. I told them to be careful of what they don't know."

"You said all this?" Mama's eyes widened.

"I did. They said they know who he is. But they believe they can handle it."

Mama went home and did not sleep that night. She did not eat. She turned this over and over in her mind, trying to understand. The government knew that Yusuf was planning for jihad and was doing nothing to try to stop him. Deep in her heart, she knew she had no power to intervene.

Meanwhile, his acolytes continued to grow in numbers, and those numbers in turn emboldened his rhetoric. He started preaching with more anger, sowing more fear that the evil West was turning Nigeria into an infidel state. This was more than a violent Salafism; it was a slow crescendo to a siren call for jihad. Yusuf's sermons started becoming more fiery, more passionate, and he was regularly repeating the same phrases from the

Qur'an, albeit with his own interpretation: "You should never lay down your weapons. Allah says, 'O believers, be on your guard; so, march in detachments or march all together.' (Q4:71) You should hold your weapons firmly and go out in small groups or as a whole. We should never lay down our weapons. I hope it is understood."[3]

Mama grew even more frustrated when the actions of Western societies added fuel to Yusuf's cause. Abu Ghraib, Guantanamo Bay, the Danish newspaper that printed a caricature of the Prophet Muhammad—every example of oppression or mal-treatment of Muslims gave Yusuf the oxygen he needed to keep the fires of Western annihilation burning.

"Look at what they are doing to Muslims in Guantanamo," he said. "Look at the Abu Ghraib prison inside Iraq. The prison was built with the money of the Iraqi people in their own land and property, yet they are the same people that are being incar-cerated in the prison. They would put people as prisoners, and a dog to assault the prisoners, while they were completely naked. They would also force a dog to sleep with the female prisoners. That is exactly what they do to people."[4]

The Ibn Taymiyyah mosque became the centre of life in Maiduguri. Mama lived close enough to it to see its transforma-tion from a gathering spot for Yusuf and his friends to a sacred space that his followers believed was ordained by Allah himself. People would drag chairs out front to listen to his sermons when there was no more capacity inside. Sometimes, Yusuf would address his followers from the entrance, using a microphone to project his voice even farther. The more extreme his rhetoric, the more concerned Mama became—and the more determined

she was to talk sense into him and her other sons. She continued to reach out, cooking big meals even as the numbers at
her gates started to dwindle. But she realized that she could no
longer compete with what Yusuf was offering. He gave the boys
money to start businesses and buy homes or cars or whatever
they wanted. He found wives for them and slaughtered cows
and goats every day, simply to create an atmosphere of celebration for his cause.

It seemed to Mama that this was all coming to a head; she just
didn't know how it would end. Yusuf was promoting jihad as
the only logical solution, the only way to confront the West and
assert sharia in Nigeria and beyond.

Looking back on this time years later, Mama could see
clearly the path to the inevitable, the confluence of factors that
transformed Yusuf's movement into one of the most dangerous
terrorist groups in the world. To his followers, Yusuf's rhetoric
came from Allah himself, and it was for Allah that they would
wage this holy war. Anyone who did not share Boko Haram's
world view was considered an infidel. Even Muslims were not
exempt—especially those who had adopted a more secular way
of life. As far as Yusuf was concerned, they had renounced their
religion. This fervent way of thinking helped set him and his
followers on a collision course with the rest of Nigerian society,
and particularly with law enforcement.

Mama also understood that the government had no good
options. In the early and mid-2000s, the Nigerian economy was
contracting, and many cities in both the south and the north

were struggling to combat a plague of petty crimes. The almajiri, now young men, were wandering the streets in groups—
some might say gangs—without jobs or prospects for the future.
Why wouldn't they steal a car or break into a home or ransack
a shop? It was easy, and it made the almajiri one of the most
feared groups in the country. Occasionally, their encounters
with authorities escalated into violence. The police—deputized
and empowered by the federal government to crack down on
petty local crimes—began making mass arrests as part of a task
force they called Operation Flush.

Mama felt a foreboding. She knew that the government was
losing patience with Yusuf and his followers, and that Operation
Flush would give them cover to finally put down his movement.
She reached out to Yusuf again, but he was long gone from her
by now. She wanted to tell him to dial down his rhetoric, to talk
to the government, to avert the confrontation she feared was
now inevitable.

But Yusuf welcomed it all, and even took pride in open defiance. "Let them come and take me!"—that was his attitude, and
it was an attitude that inspired his followers to seek martyrdom,
partly out of loyalty to their leader but mostly out of a true
belief in their cause. They saw martyrdom as the path to immor-
tality and all the treasures that awaited them in the next life.

Emboldened by their zealous belief in the one true Islam,
Boko Haram members began confronting government authorities with increasing violence. Small scuffles grew quickly into
fierce street fights. After his followers attacked a police station, Yusuf was arrested, but the charges against him didn't
stick. Authorities tried to weaken him by deporting one of his

deputies to Niger and taking others into custody, but Yusuf told his followers this was all simply harassment.

Mama's attempts to create a bridge between Boko Haram and the government became ever more futile. She believed the police were determined to teach the group a lesson and put Yusuf in his place, to prove to the rest of the country that they had the situation under control. But she also feared Yusuf's response and wondered what he might encourage his followers to do.

It wasn't long before she found out.

PART I: CAPTIVITY

1
ASMA'U AND HAUWA, 2014

ASMA'U WAS DAYDREAMING. She was in the fields with her mother and sister, picking dried leaves off the sorghum plants. The leaves were about as tall as she was, growing faster than she expected. She ran her fingers over them, checking for bugs or parasites— anything unusual that might be sucking the life out of the plants. She knew what to look for. One year, her neighbours' entire crop was destroyed by an invasion of sorghum shoot flies. They had missed the telltale long white spots on the underside of the leaves—the larvae from the eggs laid by the female. By the time they noticed the browning leaves, it was too late. A whole season's worth of work was gone.

It was a Saturday, a day off from school, and twelve-year-old Asma'u was looking forward to getting home and finishing her reading in the softening light of a languid afternoon.

"It's coming time to harvest," she overheard her mother telling her older sister, Binta. "Maybe a few more weeks."

It was just the three of them. Asma'u's younger brother and sister, Musa and Zainab, were at home with their father.

But she and Binta, who was two years older, often spent their after-school hours in the fields with their mother. Asma'u liked being in the tall sorghum plants. She loved their sweet, grassy scent and the look of the tiny flowers that held the precious seeds.

She was just picking a dead leaf off a plant when she heard her mother yell from two rows away.

"Asma'u! Binta! *Gudu, gudu.* We have to go home."

Asma'u looked up to see where her mother, Hauwa, was. Then she heard the first shots. The unmistakable sound of gunfire. She had heard it before—farmers would sometimes shoot at birds to scare them from the crops—but this was a series of shots, very sharp, very loud. Not a crack but a quick series of pops.

"Allahu Akbar!"

Asma'u froze, a sorghum leaf between her fingers. It could only be Boko Haram. Members of the terror group had been targeting villages all over Borno State, razing homes, stealing what they could—generators, goats, girls. Hauwa was now screaming at the girls to run home, about a ten-minute walk from the fields.

"Hurry!"

Asma'u caught Binta's eye. She dropped the leaf, and the girls followed their mother, dashing in and out of the plants until they reached the footpath out of the fields, then sprinted for home.

It was chaos all along the way. People were running in every direction, scattering everywhere and nowhere at once. No one knew where to go, which way would lead to refuge and which to danger. Children were crying; the elders and the lame were being carried on the backs of others.

When Hauwa and the girls got home, they found their hut a mess. Things were scattered everywhere—grass mats were over-turned, plastic chairs had been tossed about. Their father was floundering in the panic of trying to flee. He kept saying they needed papers in case they weren't able to come back. Hauwa started counting the children. The two older girls were there, yes. The two younger ones were on the floor, paralyzed with fear at seeing so much panic but unsure what everyone was so afraid of. It terrified them to see their parents in a state they didn't recognize.

"There's no time to waste. Please." Hauwa was begging her husband to leave. She could hear an airplane in the distance, then an explosion. It sounded far away, but the ground shook underneath their house. Zainab screamed. The four-year-old was afraid of loud noises, and the explosion echoed in her chest. Her six-year-old brother led her to where Asma'u was standing, and she took their small hands in hers.

For some time, there had been rumours that Boko Haram was planning to attack Gubla, a small rural community south of Maiduguri, but now that it was happening, it seemed surreal. Hauwa looked around, not knowing what to take, not knowing how long they would be gone or if they would ever be back. What if Boko Haram burned down the house, as they had so many others throughout this part of the country and beyond? She had heard of informal camps being constructed almost over-night for those who returned to their homes to find everything gone. Her mind started to race with possibilities she didn't want to think about. She could not imagine living in a camp, jammed into a small space with strangers, with no fields to tend to, no way to support the family she had worked so hard to build.

As she looked around their small house, fragments of her life came back to her in a rush. Her first husband, a fist raised against her. Suleiman, her firstborn, lost to her for years now. Then a second husband, and a chance to start again. She shook her head, as if to shake off the waves of memory that threatened to overwhelm her. She put a hand on her belly, where the promise of new life was growing. There was no time for this now.

As they left their house, Hauwa could see jet fighters circling at a distance, and she smelled smoke. Looking around, she could see a plume of grey rising from far away. It was anarchy on the roads. Cars were driving in every direction—gridlock without a grid. There were people everywhere. Babies on backs, goats in wagons. There were many ways out of town, but there was nowhere to go. Militants in pickup trucks were shooting into the air and then at the crowds, shouting, "Allahu Akbar!" They were the only ones enjoying the chaos they'd created.

Asma'u was right behind Hauwa, running as fast as she could, her little brother in tow. Binta was carrying Zainab on her back. Musa kept yelling, "Where are we going, Mama? Mama, slow down!"

They were on the road leading out of town when they heard the explosion. They all fell to the ground without thinking. Hauwa knew the blast had to have been close by. She opened her eyes and lifted her nose from the dirt. She turned her head to look back. Their home was on fire. She could see the flames, the smoke rising from the rubble.

Alhamdulillah, she thought to herself. *My house is burning.*

Where was her husband? Hauwa turned to the children. "Stay here! Stay here under this tree and do not move! I need to go back to see for myself." Before they had a chance to argue, she was gone, her long legs carrying her on instinct.

Binta and Asma'u cowered underneath the tree with their charges, watching as hundreds of others fled around them in a desperate bid to save themselves. They watched with wide and unbelieving eyes as bullets struck moving bodies, dropping them to the earth, some jerking violently before lying very still, others simply falling, a whiff of dust rising as they met the ground. None of it felt real.

They finally realized that their father was not with them. Where was he? Had he followed Hauwa back? They couldn't remember seeing him in their frantic flight, weren't sure in the mayhem of escape that he had even left the house. Men with guns seemed to be everywhere and then nowhere and then everywhere again. Asma'u and Binta exchanged glances. No words passed between them, but the questions were understood. How long should they wait for their mother? What if she forgot where she'd left them? What if she was taken on her way back? What if her body was falling to the ground somewhere?

Meanwhile, as Hauwa approached the stretch of road that led to their house, she realized she had run past death to reach it. Lifeless bodies lay on the path. Somehow, she had tricked herself into believing they were just resting as she ran by. People were yelling at her to run in the other direction. Someone told her to head for the Rock, a big hill that bordered their town. But Hauwa ran on.

Her house was still standing. It was the house behind theirs that had been reduced to a smouldering grey mass of hot ash. She ran toward it, saying a silent prayer in the hope that the neighbours had made it out. And then she saw an arm. The arm was not sticking out of the rubble; it was *on* the rubble. It was only half an arm. Hauwa raised the sleeve of her dress to her nose. She could not tell whether it was the smoke that was causing her eyes to well up or something else.

She slowed to a walk and then stopped. She could see bodies and bits of bodies scattered across what was left of the neighbours' house. There had to be at least half a dozen of them. They must have decided to stay and wait out the terrorists, only to be killed by the military bombers that had come to their defence. Her heart dropped when she realized that no one was going to save them now. She stifled an anguished scream and started to make her way back to the tree where she had left her children.

As she scrambled back, Hauwa started to regret her decision to check on the house. There were bodies everywhere. Residents fleeing and militants shooting—everything was a blur. Where had she left the children? Everywhere she turned, men with guns were yelling, shooting.

"Mama! Mama!" Hauwa saw her brood under the tree. Where was their father?

"Binta! Asma'u!" She watched in horror as a truck full of men brandishing guns drove right in front of the spot where her children were standing. She pitched forward, stumbling to reach them.

The truck rumbled ahead.

"Alhamdulillah, praise to Allah!" Hauwa said.

"Mama! Where's Papa?"

There was no time to answer.

"We must head for the Rock," Hauwa said, remembering what a stranger had yelled to her earlier.

And then they ran like they had never run in their lives. Asma'u held her younger sister's hand, gently shushing her. Her heart felt like it was about to explode. Zainab was in tears, inconsolable, terrified.

When they reached the path that led up the Rock, they met other villagers coming down.

"They won't let us pass on the other side," they explained, eyes wide with fear. "There is nowhere left for us to go."

There was a small hamlet on the other side of the Rock, and it seemed the people living there—Christians—did not want their home to be a hiding place or thoroughfare for escapees. They did not want Boko Haram targeting their village.

Hauwa and her children headed stubbornly up the path, only to be met by more people coming back down.

"They won't let us pass. We are finished. Boko Haram will find us. Alhamdulillah, where will we go? We can't go back to Gubla."

Hauwa stopped for a minute, silently cursing her husband. Where was he? Had he left the house before them? Was he lying dead somewhere, a bullet in his back and their papers in his hand?

After what seemed like forever, they finally reached the top of the Rock. A group of men stood on the path leading down the other side.

"You can't pass here, I'm sorry."

Hauwa gestured at her children. "Please," she implored. "We have nowhere to go. They will kill us."

"You can't pass through here. Go back. Go back to Boko Haram. You are all the same anyway."

"We cannot go back. Please. We're not planning on staying in your town. We just want to pass through." Hauwa was desperate.

But the men would not let them pass. By this time, others had also reached the top of the Rock and started making their own entreaties. Still, the men refused to budge.

Hauwa and her children had no choice but to turn around. Someone had mentioned a village farther away, but they had to get down from the Rock first. They joined a stream of people reluctantly turning around. When they reached the bottom, the air was humid with despair as families huddled, trying to decide which path to take.

To everyone's relief, the militants had not followed the flood of villagers along the path that led away from Gubla, so Hauwa and her children, along with countless others, went in that direction, away from the Rock and from their home.

"Mama, can we rest for a while?" Asma'u asked.

But Hauwa refused to stop. She didn't want to know what awaited them if they dared to stand still, even for a moment.

"No, we must push forward."

Asma'u wasn't sure how long they walked. All she knew was that she was desperately thirsty. They had brought a small stash of maize cakes with them, but they had no water. She thought she'd heard Hauwa say that the village was ahead when they met a group of men on the side of the road. They stopped. The men approached and pointed their guns.

"Where do you think you're going?"

"Home." Hauwa. Defiant.

"Home is the other direction, no? You can't run, lady. Wherever you go, we'll be there. We will find you. Let's make this easy on everyone and all go home together. What do you think? Back to Gubla. That's home, isn't it? In that direction?" The man laughed and nodded to the path behind them.

"Let us pass." Hauwa knew it was hopeless, but she couldn't give up so easily. They had come so far and were so close to the next village.

"Let's go." One of the men pointed a gun at Asma'u, who cowered, and then rapped the butt end on the back of her head.

She stayed silent. These men were animals. She did not want to go anywhere with them. But she was defenceless in the face of this mob. It was the first of many times Asma'u would feel powerless to defend herself, and she would look back on this as the moment she surrendered everything.

The family made the long walk back to Gubla, prodded the entire time by the ends of the militants' rifles. They tried to ignore the men's rude comments and ugly threats, desperate to outrun their own imaginations, their fears of what was to come, of what might await them at home.

Their village was smouldering. The embers were still glowing, and smoke and ash hovered, a thick fog blanketing the town. Bodies lay on the sides of roads, blood pooling around heads and torsos. Hauwa thought she heard a woman's wail, but she wondered if it was her mind giving voice to the terror in her heart. The road to their house looked strangely normal in the haze, except for the burned ruins next door.

"Where do you live?" the men asked. "Take us there."

They were getting impatient. Hauwa thought about leading them to the burned-out house, but she wondered what would happen if the men had nowhere to hold them captive. What if

Boko Haram took them into the Sambisa? She pointed to their intact home.

The men stormed in. Hauwa and the children followed.

"Who is this? Who are you?"

A man looked up.

"Papa!" The children rushed to him. Hauwa looked through her husband, as if he were an apparition. *What happened to you?* she wanted to ask, but the words would not come to her. He embraced the children but said nothing.

The gunmen observed the scene for a few minutes—father holding his children, tears of relief at being reunited, but everyone shaking in fear of what would happen next. The men acted quickly. They shoved the children out of the way and used the ends of their guns to separate their father from them. Then two of them grabbed him by the arms and dragged him out of the house.

"Where are you taking him?" Binta was screaming now. "Don Allah! Please! Wayyo Allah! Please stop!" Binta's voice became high and frantic.

Hauwa stood speechless as her eldest daughter stamped her feet on the floor. Words failed to form in her mind.

"Shut up!" One of the gunmen decided he had heard enough and slapped Binta across the face with such force that she fell backwards.

"Let's go," another said, and hauled her out of the house as well.

Asma'u stifled a cry that was threatening to explode out of her body. Finally, Hauwa could not be silent any longer. She started screaming, "Binta, Binta! Don Allah, don Allah!" She was no longer in her own body, in her own mind. She ran through the home, yelling unintelligible words and flailing her fists in the air.

"She's gone crazy. Maybe she has always been crazy." Asma'u overheard the gunmen talking. "Shut up, woman. It's over. This house belongs to us now. Everything belongs to us now."

But Hauwa continued her rampage. She was now screaming nonsense. Because nothing made sense.

The gunmen turned to Asma'u. "Control her. Do not try to leave. We will be back. If you are not here, we will hunt you down and kill you. Consider yourself lucky that we have not taken your head today."

They left without another word.

Asma'u doesn't remember how long they were in that house. She does remember trying to clean up a little bit after Hauwa's ranting. She remembers finding the papers her father had stayed behind to look for. She remembers seeing her mother stone-faced, rocking back and forth, muttering to herself, rubbing her belly, apologizing to her unborn child.

Their food stores were bare—the militants had taken it all. They had nothing but the maize cakes they'd brought with them on their escape to nowhere. The cakes were crushed now, having been tossed about as the family was fleeing from one place to another. Asma'u spread them on the floor, reshaping them, then fed them to her younger siblings. She held a piece out to her mother, but Hauwa could not eat. She knew she should be feeding the child inside her, but she couldn't bring herself to put anything in her mouth. She pushed the dry cake away but then reached for her daughter's fingers, holding them firmly, as if to apologize for not taking sustenance from her. And for everything that was happening to them. Squeezing Asma'u's hand, she closed her eyes and tried to imagine that this was all a horrible nightmare, that she would wake up and her husband and eldest daughter would walk through the entrance. She felt the baby move inside her.

She took a piece of the cake from Asma'u. Eventually, exhaustion overtook her and she closed her eyes.

Asma'u ventured outside to see what was happening in the village. There was a man with a gun—a guard, presumably—posted on the road leading to their house. There was no way to get out without being spotted. She suddenly remembered that she'd left a basin of water around the back of the house before they fled. She went around, only to find it overturned, just as everything else had been.

Later that day, a guard dropped off some water and a bag of flour ground from millet—the family's allotment. Asma'u gathered some sticks and found the matches her father had stored under a rock, then made a small fire in the back. The militants had not taken everything, and Asma'u whispered a prayer of gratitude for the small iron pot that remained outside. She poured in some of the flour but saved most of it because she didn't know when more would arrive. She added water and set the mix over the fire, stirring with a dirty spoon until it thickened into something that resembled a weak pudding. When it cooled, she brought it to her younger brother and sister, giving them turns with the spoon. When they'd had their fill, she held the spoon out to her mother. Hauwa shook her head. Asma'u decided to leave the pot next to her, in case she changed her mind later on.

After everyone had gone to sleep, she again ventured outside. This time, she saw several gunmen standing in the entrance of a house nearby. They were chewing khat leaves, gnawed on as a stimulant, and talking among themselves in the waxing light of a gibbous moon.

One of the men spoke in a low voice. "The army is coming to take back the town. The amir says we need to leave."

Another man looked skeptical. "Do we know when they are coming?"

"The amir heard that it will be soon. We need to be ready." The first man lowered his voice even more, but he was met with derision.

"Ready for what?" the second man scoffed. "Those soldiers with their fancy weapons? They are no match for us. They will come again with the planes and bombs. Ha! Their bombs kill more people than Boko Haram."

Asma'u tiptoed back inside and roused her mother, who had slumped over on the floor of the main room. She whispered into Hauwa's ear, "Mama, the army is coming. We'll be free from the bad men very soon."

Hauwa opened her eyes but didn't move. She didn't care anymore if the army came. She didn't care if she had to live under Boko Haram rules forever. She wanted her daughter back. Her husband. Her life.

"Mama, Boko Haram is going to leave, and the army will find Papa and Binta. Don't worry."

Hauwa closed her eyes and pictured herself holding Binta again. She would hold on to her with all she had and never let go.

When several men stormed into the house the next morning, Asma'u thought they were soldiers coming to tell them they had chased Boko Haram out of town. Her heart sank when she recognized one of them as the guard from the day before. She reached for Zainab and Musa, rousing them from their sleep. Hauwa gathered all of them to her and lowered her eyes. The men were yelling now.

"*Yi sauri!* Hurry! Everyone come with us. There is no time to waste." They pushed the barrels of their weapons against Hauwa's shoulder. "Move."

Hauwa did not budge.

"Mama." For a second, Asma'u feared her mother would be killed for defying their orders. But then Hauwa looked at her children and reluctantly let herself be led out the door and into the back of a pickup truck.

Soon, they were rumbling down the road out of Gubla, leaving behind a town in ruins and countless human bodies in fields, in homes, on the roads. Left to return to the earth on their own. The truck joined another and another, until a convoy snaked away from the wreckage, a cloud of dust in its wake.

As she held on to her younger sister and brother, crammed together in the back of the truck, Asma'u started to cry. One of the men shouted at her to stop.

"Shut up! Are you a baby? No. Stop your crying."

It made her cry even harder. She knew—had heard—about Boko Haram's extreme cruelty; a friend from school had told her about it after her relatives in another town were forced to live under the group's occupation until the military chased them out. To Asma'u, it seemed like a nightmare that had now become all too real. How could anyone be this cruel to children? She was only twelve. Zainab and Musa were four and six.

One of the men rapped her with his gun.

"I told you to shut up. Stop your crying."

"Don't touch her!" Hauwa was angry. How dare they hit her daughter? How dare they talk to her in this way? Her fury was met with the butt end of a rifle. And then one of the men raised his gun and shot into the air.

"Shut up. I will only say this once."

It was nearly sundown when the convoy finally stopped. It felt like they had been driving for hours, and Hauwa's back was hurting from the tossing and jouncing on the journey. She put a hand on her abdomen to reassure the child inside, afraid that he or she would feel the chills that shook her entire body. Because she had suddenly realized where they were. The Sambisa. The home of Boko Haram.

The gunmen flipped open the back of the truck and ordered everyone out. Others were doing the same at the vehicles that had arrived just ahead of them. The militants corralled their hostages into a semicircle at the entrance to the camp. Hauwa could see makeshift huts, some with tarps for roofs, others with pieces of corrugated metal salvaged from somewhere. It had the feel of a village or a camp for displaced persons, the kind people built for themselves after Boko Haram destroyed their homes. Small cooking fires burned everywhere, and Hauwa could smell maize pudding simmering nearby. She hadn't eaten in more than a day, but the smell of it turned her stomach. Then her eyes widened.

"Where is my husband? Is my daughter here? Where are they? Take us to them."

The gunmen laughed. One of them spit on the ground next to her.

"You stupid woman. You are all on your own here. They could be here or they could be at another camp. This is not the only camp in the forest. Don't you know anything? Your husband, if he is a real man, has already joined us and is out taking more villages with the soldiers."

"He is nothing like you, you dirty pigs." Hauwa's indignation earned her a slap across the face.

"You will find out soon enough."

Asma'u had had the same thought when they arrived at the camp. Immediately, she had started to scan her surroundings for any sign of her father and sister. She thought she saw a girl who looked like Binta stoking a fire nearby, but the girl wore a head covering and Asma'u couldn't really see her features. She took a few steps away from the group, trying to catch a glimpse of her face. Then the girl turned her head, revealing one eye that was swollen shut and a bruise that stretched all the way down to the bottom of her cheekbone. For a split second, she looked into Asma'u's staring eyes, then she quickly covered her face with her scarf and turned away. Asma'u shuddered. The girl could not have been much older than she was, certainly no older than Binta. How long had she been here? What was she doing here? She looked worn, old, empty. A cold drop of fear ran down Asma'u's spine as she wondered whether she was looking into some future version of herself.

Just then, a loud voice started speaking to the new arrivals.

"Women, here." The man they called the amir pointed to one side of the semicircle where the group had been corralled. "Take your children with you. Everyone else, here." He pointed to the open space behind him.

Asma'u followed her mother, holding one sibling by each hand.

"You. Here." Another voice boomed from behind.

Mother and daughter both turned around. A man grabbed Asma'u by the arm and dragged her over to the other group.

"No!" Hauwa screamed. "She is just a child."

Asma'u froze, staring at her mother. She clung to Hauwa's arm. The man took his knife and held it between them, and suddenly a stream of blood ran down both their arms. Asma'u screamed.

"Stop," Hauwa pleaded. "Wayyo Allah. Please stop. She has to come with me."

Musa and Zainab realized what was happening, and they both started screaming Asma'u's name.

The amir looked at Asma'u. Up and down. Up and down. She wanted to shrink inside herself, so conscious was she of his eyes lingering on her changing body. She bowed her head so he wouldn't be able to see her big dark eyes and the full lips she'd inherited from her mother.

The amir finished his appraisal and then looked straight into Hauwa's pleading eyes. "This girl is no longer yours. She now belongs to Baba Shekau."

Baba Shekau. Baba Shekau. Abubakar Shekau. The feared, loathed leader of Boko Haram.

Hauwa let out a guttural wail from somewhere deep and dark as Asma'u was led away by two of the amir's men. Everything went black as Hauwa fell to the ground.

2
GAMBO, 2013

GAMBO WAS GATHERING dry sticks, stray bits of twigs and branches, then breaking them off with her hands and piling them up between a few rocks in preparation for the evening's fire, which would fuel the family's meal that night. Afternoon prayers had just finished, and it was time to think about supper. Rice and pepper soup, perhaps. She would have to check with her mother to see what they could add to the pot. Hajera knew what was in the family's stores and what was not. But there was little to keep track of, really. Food had been scarce of late. Boko Haram's attacks on neighbouring villages and farms had driven many people away; others had been killed, left lifeless in the fields that they had tended so carefully for most of their days.

But for now, Gambo tucked away her thoughts of Boko Haram, even though this required more effort with each passing day because there was a constant stream of news about attacks on this village just over there or that village so close by. She struck a precious match, holding the flame to the twigs. The loose mound of wood started to smoke, and she blew on it to help the fire catch. Then she picked up a thatched fan and waved it with a quick wrist at the base, still wondering what else she could put in the soup. She turned her head away from the smoke, her eyes watering.

She heard gunfire.

And then shouts of "Allahu Akbar!"

"They are here!"

She thought she saw her brother running in front of her, but then everyone was running and yelling. "They" could only mean Boko Haram. "*Gudu!* Run!" A cacophony of frightened voices, calling out to children, to parents, to anyone. People gathering their families, wondering where to go, which direction to flee. People everywhere. The sound of children crying, the dust circling the air as people ran. Possessions strewn about as if an earthquake had shaken the foundations of life in peaceful Gulak. And then the sound of gunshots seemed to get louder. Trucks full of men, men with guns, guns pointed in the air, the air cracking open with bullets that seemed to be flying in all directions.

Gambo sat there for a time, staring into the fire she was trying to start. It might have been only a minute, but in that moment, she felt paralyzed. She sensed there was a line being drawn, a shift in the world. She had heard about this, how Boko Haram splits your life, and your soul, into a before and an after.

"Gambo!" Her mother was shouting at her to move. Hajera was rounding up her other children—Gambo's younger brothers and sister—and gathering what she could. The gunfire was louder now. Gambo imagined people being shot—her neighbours, her schoolmates—and finally she left her fire to follow her mother. Where could they run to? How could they hide? People were shouting for them to run to Mubi, a town directly to the south. Others were heading to the mountains to the east of Gulak. Some simply retreated to their mud huts, trying to convince themselves that their modest homes would offer them a degree of protection.

Gambo followed her siblings and her mother. They joined an endless flow of people now running along the main road past the town's market and south toward Mubi. It was dusty and hot, and with the crack of bullets in the air, people were ducking and diving as they fled. The acrid smell of fear permeated the atmosphere as the residents of Gulak ran for their lives in their sandals, their worn sneakers, their bare feet.

Eventually, the running slowed, the gunfire stopped, homes faded into the distance and into the twilight. It was getting dark, and the group—perhaps dozens of mostly women and children—needed somewhere to rest for the night. Someone mentioned a village ahead, and the group trudged forward, hoping to settle before dark. No one seemed to know where they were. They were still a fair distance from Mubi, but they needed to rest. They entered the small village—more like a hamlet, really—and dispersed, finding shelter in abandoned huts, under trees, behind mud walls, wherever they could. They might have collapsed from exhaustion and the burnout of adrenaline, but they were too frightened that Boko Haram would track them down, as they were known to do.

Gambo stayed close to her mother and siblings; she and her eleven-year-old sister, Asta, three years her junior, held each other. She said a silent prayer for their safety through the night and then felt her eyelids becoming heavy. She readjusted her headscarf and closed her eyes. Her thoughts drifted to her father. She tried to conjure up his image, but he was fading from her with each year. A truck driver who'd delivered goods all through Borno and Adamawa, he was killed in an accident when Gambo was only eight. She wondered how things might be different if he were still alive.

She heard a soft male voice at first. And then others chimed in. "Boko Haram won't hurt you. You can go back to Gulak."

Gambo wasn't sure if she was dreaming, but just in case, she willed herself awake. By the time she'd opened her eyes, she could see in the dark distance a small group with a young boy at the centre.

"It's true," said the boy. "Boko Haram doesn't want to kill you. Gulak is safe. If you want, you can go back to get your things."

People murmured that they didn't believe the boy, that Boko Haram was setting a trap. But one woman said she wanted to go back to check on her neighbours. Another wanted to retrieve something of value. Someone else warned them not to listen to such nonsense. "This boy is one of them."

Gambo sat up. Asta stirred next to her, an arm still around her sister's waist. Gambo couldn't tell if her mother was asleep. Hajera's back was to her, but she could see the rise and fall of her breath underneath her scarf. She knew her mother would want to go back. They had left too much behind. They had left everything behind.

She nudged her mother's back and whispered that people were saying it was safe to go home. Boko Haram isn't out to kill us, she said. Hajera stirred and opened one eye.

"We can go," Gambo said. "*Gida*." Home.

It was now dawn. Gambo looked around at the village—a few thatched huts and a couple of dirt roads leading to a few more thatched huts. She scanned the area for a water pump but couldn't see one. Already some people were rousing themselves out of whatever sleep they were able to get, shaking off the dust and chaff that clung to their clothes, and walking slowly back toward the road that had led them here just a few hours earlier. Hajera nodded and shook Gambo's brothers awake. They would follow.

It had been at least half a day since any of them had even a sip of water, and the boys were crying out of thirst and hunger. But there would be no relief—at least not yet, not until they got home.

Gambo and Asta held hands as they walked behind their mother and brothers, wondering what was awaiting them. They had left their village in such a rush. Her fire would have gone out by now. But what she knew about Boko Haram—what they did when they went into villages and raided and razed—rattled around like stones in her mind. Maybe their home had been burned to the ground. Maybe their neighbours had been killed. What would be left for them to gather?

They had not gone very far when they saw people running toward them just as they themselves had fled the day before. "*Gudu!*" They turned around to head back to the other village, hiding under a tree next to a mud wall. But it was too late. Boko Haram was suddenly upon them, shooting indiscriminately. Asta's fingers tightened around Gambo's hand, and Gambo gave her a squeeze. People were screaming, crying.

"*Tsaya!* Stop!" Gambo looked at the hut where they had spent the night and saw blood seeping out from underneath it. Almost immediately, there seemed to be bodies everywhere, people falling and yelling out. "*Taimake ni!* Help!" It was more chaotic than the day before, when the men had entered Gulak. The rat-a-tat-tat of gunfire seemed endless. A sulphurous, metallic smell filled the air. *This is what death must smell like*, Gambo thought. She said a prayer in her head and closed her eyes, waiting for the bullet that would put an end to this. *Inshallah*.

Then the shooting stopped. Gambo looked up to see men pointing their guns at people, rounding up those they had not killed in their crazed rampage. There were maybe a few dozen—the spared—and she wondered if she wore the same dazed expression she saw all around her. Asta looked at her, wordlessly. What now?

The spared were now the captured, a line of prisoners being marched back to Gulak. They were flanked by fighters brandishing semi-automatic weapons and others in the back of pickup trucks, ensuring that no one could escape.

Gambo held her sister's hand and adjusted her headscarf, eyes downcast, fearful of accidentally meeting the gaze of a fighter. It was too late—she could feel eyes on her and she pulled her sister closer.

"What's your name? Pretty one here. Maybe they'll give you to me when we get to the forest."

"No, I bet she goes to Shekau. Look at her. Tall and pretty. Two of them. One for me, one for Shekau." The man's voice managed to be both mocking and menacing.

Gambo clutched Asta's arm, and they hastened their steps. She suddenly felt exposed in a way that made the blood rush up her neck and flush her face. She wished she could disappear, come apart at the soul and scatter like fine dust into the dirt on the road.

The sisters had inherited their mother's statuesque form and her wide-set, piercing dark eyes. Gambo also had her high cheekbones, accentuating her almond-shaped eyes. Full lips were not uncommon among women here, but her thin jaw was. The combination made her stand out; in another life, she could have easily graced the cover of *Vogue* and walked the catwalk for the biggest fashion houses in the world. But for the grace of God. Alhamdulillah.

She quickened her steps, almost dragging Asta with her and passing her mother and brothers in an effort to put some distance between them and the fighters. Up ahead, gunshots rang out and a collective shudder shook the group. Furtive glances to assure themselves that family members and fellow travellers were still with them. Ahead, riotous laughter could be heard from one of the pickup trucks.

"Run away," a voice called out. "Just try. See what happens, eh!"

When the cloud of dust settled behind the truck, Gambo could make out two bodies by the side of the road. A man was missing half his face. A woman was face down in the dirt.

The callousness was shocking. The men were laughing. After having executed two innocent people for the crime of trying to get away.

As they approached Gulak, the smell of burning was unmistakable. The pace picked up as the ragged line of tired prisoners pressed forward to see what had become of their town, their homes.

"Don't even try to leave," one man warned. "Go to your houses, but do not leave the village. We all live here now, and this is our territory. You will do what we say. You will follow our rules."

Gambo's home was still there. The thatched hut had escaped the worst of it. A neighbour came to them, crying about a dead husband and a home destroyed. Hajera's normally calm and measured voice shook just a little as she told the woman she could stay with them.

Gambo took in everything around her. She could hear the distant wailing of the newly widowed. The cries of hungry children. The yelling and heavy-booted footfalls of their occupiers. Then she noticed the fire she'd left behind. It had never taken. She rearranged the sticks and searched for a match.

The next morning, the soldiers went from hut to hut, home to home, forcing everyone out at gunpoint, then marching them toward the mosque in the middle of town. By the time Gambo and her family had staggered there, there might have been a couple of hundred people standing around, all looking shell-shocked, lives upended in an instant. Men with guns surrounded the villagers. Gambo wondered if they were all about to be executed. Then a man they called the amir started speaking. It was obvious he was in charge.

"You will not leave this village, do you understand? If you try to leave, we will kill you. Do you understand? You will do what we say. If you don't, we will kill you. This is our village now, and you will live under our rules."

No one dared speak. After more threats, people were allowed to go back to their homes, with the understanding that they would stay there under house arrest. They lived this way for weeks, settling into a different kind of normal. Mosque attendance was mandatory, as were Islamic studies. Imams taught a version of fundamentalist Islam that scared even the most conservative Muslims in the community. It was the only form of education allowed. Regular school was *haram*, or forbidden. No more history classes or Hausa language classes, and definitely no English classes. No gathering after sundown. Headscarves were mandatory for women. And yet, Gambo considered herself lucky. She had not been moved into a house with other women, nor was she married off to a Boko Haram fighter. She knew of other girls her age, and even younger, who had been forced to live with their fighter husbands.

So she kept a low profile, staying mostly in their hut, save for the time spent in the Islamic classes. She and her mother and siblings were hungry all the time. Everyone had been forced to give up their stores of food, and then the amir reallocated it in small portions. There was never enough. The men in the village were forced to join the fighters in their attempt to take Mubi, a larger city two hours south in Adamawa State. Some who refused were shot on the spot. Others were called to the school, where the militants slit their throats and took their heads. Boko Haram didn't have time for anyone who didn't follow their instructions.

The women were horrified, howling. But they were forced to help take the bodies into the bush, where the fighters had dug a mass grave.

It didn't take long for bodies to spill out of the pit.

One day, when Gambo went to the well for fresh water, she overheard two women talking. The army was about to come and drive out Boko Haram, they said. She wanted to know more.

"How do you know this?" she asked.

"It's what all the men are whispering about." The amir, they said, had been making plans. And so the women were also making plans. It might be a good opportunity to escape. When the fighting started, they could use the back road leading into the bush.

Gambo went home with her pail of water and excitedly told her mother what she'd heard.

Hajera was quiet for a while, absorbing this information. She scooped water out of the pail, pouring it into a basin full of dusty corn kernels. She stirred the kernels to wash them, then poured the silty water out, replenishing the basin with fresh scoops from the pail. She repeated the process twice more, letting the water drain from her fingers as she cradled the precious kernels in her palms and continued to think about Gambo's information, turning it over and over in her mind until it became as clear as the fresh water in the pail.

That night, after darkness had fallen, Hajera decided they should leave at once, to avoid being caught in the crossfire or becoming human shields for their captors. And so they walked—slowly at first—down a road, the five of them, taking almost nothing with them. They would come back after the army had freed the town.

They were on the outskirts of Gulak, heading toward the mountains to the east, when they heard the wheels of a car scrabbling along the dirt road behind them. Gambo froze on the spot. Had they been followed?

"Hajera. Gambo," a man's voice whispered. It was Hajera's brother-in-law, her late husband's brother. "Get in," he said, and the back doors of his old clunker swung open. His three children and wife were hunkered down. How could there be room for five more? But somehow they managed.

Hajera shut the door quietly and firmly against her leg, and Gambo's uncle continued the car's slow crawl to safety. No one spoke as they drove east on the road next to the hills. The car picked up speed once they were clear of Gulak. Gambo looked out the window and could see the outline of a farm with a drift of pigs grazing on chaff. She took a breath. Her heart started to return to its regular beat, and she willed herself to close her eyes. She didn't know where they were going, but she felt a lightness she thought she had forgotten.

Then the car stalled and stopped. Gambo's uncle tried to restart it, but it seemed as if the engine had died. He turned the key in the ignition over and over to no avail, trying not to panic as he glanced nervously in the rear-view mirror. Gambo opened her eyes; she really didn't know how much time had passed since they stalled. It was light out now. They were next to a farm where Gambo could see pigs penned behind a fence.

All at once, she saw that their stalled car was surrounded. Several men were pointing guns inside. Was this real? Was she dreaming? She felt like she was being suffocated. She had a fleeting thought that the pigs had more freedom than she did.

One of the men stuck his head inside the front passenger window. "Where are you going?" he asked in a sing-songy voice that sounded more threatening than friendly.

No one responded.

The man chortled. "We are everywhere, you know. There is no escaping." He took a step back from the car and set his gaze on the pigpen Gambo had been focused on.

He lifted his gun, and without warning, he fired. And fired. Gambo could hear the sound of pigs squealing, trapped in their pen, running, crying. The other men joined in. The car jolted and its passengers ducked, trying to shield their ears from the deafening sounds.

"*Kafirai!* Infidels!"

As the men rushed to the pen, guns blazing, the farmer ran out, yelling at them to stop. He looked stooped and old to Gambo, and seemed to wince in pain with every step he took. The men shot indiscriminately. Within seconds, the farmer was on the ground, unmoving, blood pouring from his head, his torso. Dead pigs were everywhere. Blood was everywhere.

Gambo's uncle turned from the front seat. "*Gudu!*" The doors of the sedan flung open and the passengers poured out. Gambo was holding Asta's hand again, as she had from the beginning. Hajera had one of the boys on her back and a hand clutching the other. They ducked as they ran, bracing for the bullet that would kill them. They ran into the hills, not looking behind, not wanting to know if the gunmen were chasing, if the bullets were close.

Eventually, they realized that the men had not followed them. They collapsed where they stood. The sun was rising on another uncertain day. They settled against the trunks of some trees. No one spoke for ages. It was understood that they could not remain here. They had no water, no food. And it was a long walk back to Gulak.

Gambo started to scratch the back of her hand. The beginning of another rash. She wasn't sure what brought these rashes on, but they had plagued her for as long as she could remember. A village "doctor" had once diagnosed her with stomach worms—that was his explanation for these periodic red flashes that would ravage her skin and drive her mad with their stinging and itching. She once fainted during Eid when she saw that her body was covered in red spots. Her mother revealed that she was a sickly baby and had refused to feed at her breast.

It was another excuse for her father not to send her to school. But just an excuse—she knew he didn't believe that girls should be educated. There was never any question that her younger brothers would go to school, and as soon as they were old enough, they did, leaving their sisters at home. Gambo wondered what her father would have done if he were with them now, on the run from Boko Haram. He would probably have tried to take them out of Gulak, just as her uncle had done.

After Hajera's own father died, she moved the children to Gulak to live with her side of the family. Gambo's uncle asked why she and Asta were not in school, and that's when the girls were finally enrolled, years behind their classmates. Gambo liked school. She was just finishing level 2 of junior school, or the equivalent to eighth grade. One more year and then it was off to senior school. She would graduate a few years later and had always imagined she would move to a bigger city—like Yola, the capital of Adamawa State—to find a job. She didn't want to stay in Gulak forever. They had just been about to go on school break when the militants took over their town. She missed school. The Islamic classes their occupiers forced them to attend were not the same.

Gambo kept scratching her hand. And then she felt a familiar stinging at the nape of her neck. And on her leg.

Two days later, the small group decided they had likely outlasted the terrorists. It seemed safe to go back to the car they had abandoned next to the farm where the pigs and the farmer had been slaughtered. But when they finally reached it, they found a black metal frame, the smell of smoke still lingering around it. Boko Haram had destroyed the sedan.

They had little choice but to risk the long walk back to the village. If they were lucky, the military would have chased out the militants by now. But they would soon find out that there had been no raid. Not yet. At the outskirts of town, Gambo's uncle told them to wait while he went ahead to see if it was safe to proceed. When he didn't return, his wife told Hajera she would go to look for him and send word back as soon as she could.

It felt like hours. Gambo was scratching her arm when she heard a rustle of footsteps and then a deep wail that seemed to come from some dark place.

"*Ya mutu!* He's gone!"

Hajera ran forward, just in time to catch her sister-in-law as she fell to her knees, her sobs shaking everyone around them. Then her children started to cry, and they threw themselves on top of their mother, all of them shaking, the foundation of their family suddenly gone. Gambo felt numb. Maybe it was because of exhaustion from the walk, or shock at how swiftly death could come, or delirium from the itching and stinging of her skin. Whatever the reason, she was unable to muster any tears. Her aunt was now running back toward the village, children in tow, in a desperate effort to bury her husband before the militants disposed of his body.

Gambo looked at her mother. Hajera shook her head: they had no choice but to follow. There was nowhere else to go.

Not much had changed in Gulak in the few days they were in the mountains. If Boko Haram had been preparing for an imminent confrontation with the military, there was little evidence of that. Food was so scarce that people were drinking the water they used to wash their meagre corn rations. Everyone seemed to be praying for the much-rumoured raid to come. *Alhamdulillah! It will be soon.*

And then, just as suddenly as the militants had swooped in to take over the town, they rounded up their remaining captives—

Gambo and her family, her aunt and her children, all the women and children left in Gulak. Their pickup trucks created a dust storm as they drove out of town, loaded down with their hostages, heading into the Sambisa forest.

3
THE FOREST

GAMBO

They got to the forest just as dawn was breaking. They knew that's where they were going, but it was still a shock to arrive in the middle of the Sambisa. The gunmen opened the back of the truck, and Gambo and her family slid out at gunpoint. Asta was still clinging to her arm, as she had the entire ride. But almost immediately, they were separated. Her mother, aunt, and siblings all on one side. Gambo and a few other girls around her age on another.

One of the men approached her. "Here. Take this. A gift from me to you." Gambo looked down. In his grubby, stubby outstretched hand was a succulent brown *dabino*, a perfect specimen of a date. She looked back up at the man who held it out to her. She knew what a gift this small sweet fruit was. In her family, dates were reserved for special occasions. He watched her as she contemplated whether to take it from him. But her hunger got the better of her. She took it and devoured it in a few quick bites.

"Very good," the man said, smiling. "I'm so happy you enjoyed it. There are more where that one came from."

Another man—the others called him Baba Laba—stepped forward and addressed the new arrivals. Gambo and Hajera would soon learn that he was much feared as Abubakar Shekau's deputy. His voice echoed through the forest. "You are in our custody now. Do you hear me? Do not try to leave the forest. If you do, you will get lost trying to find the way out. And we will find you and kill you. Do not believe we won't. We have killed many others who tried to leave. You belong to us now."

Gambo was led away with the other young women she had been grouped with. They would be housed together in a make-shift shack. Meanwhile, Hajera and the rest of her children, along with the others, were led away in another direction.

"This is Camp One," bellowed the man who had given the date to Gambo. "This is your home now."

Hajera looked around. She saw several huts and some people sleeping under trees with a tarp stretched over several sticks. She settled against a tree trunk and motioned for the children to gather around her.

"Where is Gambo?" Asta was distraught.

Hajera smoothed her hair as if to reassure them both that Gambo was okay wherever she was, but she was shaking. She didn't want to imagine where her daughter was or what the gunmen were doing to her.

A woman who had made camp under a blue tarp not far from Hajera walked over to them with a jug of water. "Here, take this. Tomorrow I will show you where you get more, and where to get food. Where are you from?"

Hajera opened her mouth, but no words came out. Despite

her best efforts, they had ended up in the very place they sought so hard to avoid.

"*Nagode*," she finally whispered to the woman. "Thank you."

The women spoke quietly for a time, and Hajera learned that Amina was from Gwoza, north of their home village of Gulak and closer to the border with Cameroon. Amina had been at the camp for several weeks with her three younger children. Two older daughters were separated from her upon arrival, just as Gambo had been. Amina spoke to Hajera in a low voice, just above a whisper.

"You can see them sometimes when you are getting food and water. They were forced to marry fighters. They don't talk much about it. But you can plan to meet there at the same time every day or every few days. Or sometimes you will see them during Islamic lessons—they hold them under the baobab tree in the clearing. There's not much else we do here but wait for our chance to leave. When the military launches an operation, that's the time. Just make sure you know the way out."

Gambo's first night in the forest was spent in a clearing. She and several other girls had been led there by a tall man carrying a big gun. They were forced to take off their colourful wrappers and were given dark mayafis to put on instead. The girls looked around. Disrobing in front of an audience of sneering men with guns was deeply discomforting. At home, Gambo had never even undressed in front of her siblings, and here there wasn't so much as a tree to hide behind. She could feel eyes on her as she unwrapped her dress and slid the mayafi over her head.

Heat rose up her neck and into her cheeks. The other girls did the same, hurriedly. When they were done, their wrappers were taken away and they were left on their own.

"You will sleep here tonight. We are just over there. We will see you if you try to leave. And we will shoot you if you do."

The men then walked back in the direction of the camp. The girls stared at each other, not daring to move. Finally, when it seemed clear that no one was coming back, Gambo sat down, and the rest of the girls followed her lead. The ground was still warm from the heat of the day, and the air was humid with tears and sweat. At first, no one spoke. And then someone said out loud the words that were ringing in all of their minds: "What are they going to do with us? Where are our families?"

There were no answers in the dark. Or perhaps, fear kept them from being imagined out loud.

Thoughts of what might await them in the morning prevented Gambo from closing her eyes. But soon, the sound of rustling made her wonder what was waiting for them here, in the forest. The rustling sounded like someone, or something, pushing back leaves in the bush, but there were no footsteps, and her mind started to wander through possibilities. What was causing the noise? Or more precisely, what creatures were they sharing this space with? She had heard of poisonous snakes slithering along the forest floor, killing at will, even swallowing whole birds and small animals. And she also remembered hearing about large crab-like spiders that crawled up trees looking for food. She hugged her knees closer to her chest, trying to make herself smaller.

The sound of muffled sobbing interrupted her thoughts. It was one of the other girls, curled up in a tiny ball a few feet away from Gambo. She was younger and had slightly fairer skin. She reminded Gambo a little of Asta, only a bit older. She had seen the girl get pushed out of a vehicle ahead of hers when they arrived at the camp. She wished she could say something to comfort her, wished she could go over and reassure her with a hand on her shoulder, but she felt paralyzed. Gambo couldn't bring herself to lie and give the girl the reassurance she needed.

Darkness slowly gave way to dawn, which announced itself with birdsong that seemed out of place in their circumstances. Gambo closed her eyes and tried to imagine she was anywhere else—back home in her village, taking a break from her schoolwork; in the playground at her junior school, listening to the younger children sing. Anywhere but where she was. Some of the other girls were getting up and heading deeper into the bush to relieve themselves, but Gambo felt too anxious, her body too tense. Besides, she'd had nothing to drink for at least twenty-four hours, so there was no need. She stretched her long legs out in front of her.

Just as the girls returned from the bush, two men with guns approached the clearing, motioning with the barrels for the girls to gather.

"You lucky girls," said one of the men. "You are all getting married." He was scornful and lewd and spoke with glee.

Gambo's chest tightened. She was not getting married. She did not want to get married. She hadn't even started senior high school.

"If you do not marry, you will martyr. You want to marry? Or you want to go to Jannat?"

Gambo wanted to ask what awaited women and girls in heaven if all those virgins were already betrothed to male martyrs. But she maintained her silence. Some of the girls were shaking their heads no—they did not want to marry. But no one found the courage to speak.

"You and you, come with me," said one of the men, tapping Gambo and the girl she had heard crying in the clearing with his gun. "The rest of you, do not try to leave. Do you understand? It will be your turn in time."

The others looked on as the men led Gambo and the girl back into the bush, down a rough path, and past a few huts. The other girl looked to be on the verge of tears again.

"Where is he taking us?" she whispered to Gambo.

Gambo couldn't answer. She was trying to figure out whether they were passing the same huts she had seen the night before, or whether this path led them deeper into the forest.

Several minutes later, they arrived at another clearing with a three-sided hut. Several women were there already, hacking away at a large goat on a table that looked like it might have once belonged in a school. There was blood on the ground around them, and shards of bone and bits of flesh were splattered everywhere.

"This is where you'll work."

The women looked at Gambo and the girl. One of them handed Gambo a knife and motioned for her to get to work. She could barely butcher a chicken, let alone a goat, but she followed the lead of the women and started to work on one of the legs. The meat was put in a pile at a corner of the long table; bones went to the opposite corner.

Gambo's hands were soon covered in blood, but she didn't care, not at all. She dug her fingers deeper into the flesh, as if finishing off the goat was a kind of release. She smelled a fire and realized there was a large pit behind the hut. Two women and the young girl who had come with Gambo were fanning the flames under a large pot at least two times bigger than the one they had at home. Ifeoma, the woman who had handed Gambo the knife, scooped up the pile of bones, walked over to the fire, and dumped them into the pot. One of the other women nodded to the girl, who then took a jug of water and poured it over the bones.

Gambo's gaze fell upon a pile of leaves. She guessed they were from the baobab tree she had passed on her way to the cooking hut, and after a few minutes, the girl dumped them into the pot as well. One of the women picked up a big spoon and started stirring.

Gambo continued her work, cutting the meat into pieces. She learned that Ifeoma had been at the camp for several months, and that she had been separated from her children and husband when Boko Haram attacked their village. Here in the forest, she was living with several other women and was basically in service to the wives of the commanders.

"If you marry a commander," she whispered to Gambo, "life here can be bearable. But you may have to give up a piece of your soul."

Gambo replied that she didn't want to get married. Not to a commander. Not to a fighter. Not to anyone.

"It's no longer your choice," the older woman told her. "It's best to do what they say."

Gambo soon found out why that was probably the best advice for living in the forest. The punishment for refusing to do what you were told was always corporal, often public, and sometimes deadly. Her first week in the forest, she witnessed floggings, beatings, beheadings, and shootings. Mostly it was people who had tried to leave the camp. Escape was an offence punishable by death. Gambo quickly became familiar with the way a body in a dark mayafi slumped to the ground, like a rag doll folding in on itself. It was shocking how easy it was for life to be snuffed out.

A boy perhaps a few years younger than Gambo was caught trying to leave the camp one morning. At midday, everyone was summoned to the mosque area, which was just an open expanse under a big baobab tree. The boy was marched out. His hands were tied behind his back, and he was forced to kneel. And then the amir strode out and made a speech.

"You will all see now what happens to those who try to leave. Why would you want to leave?" His tone turned mocking. "This is not a bad place. We feed you. We clothe you. You have everything you need. You, boy, why did you have to do this?" He was yelling now, spitting out every angry word.

The yelling continued as the amir circled around the bound boy. Gambo noticed that the boy's legs were shaking. The amir then pulled out a knife—a big one, bigger than the one Gambo's mother used to butcher her chickens, bigger than the one she herself had used on the goat. The long blade of the knife caught the sun as the amir waved it around, and the flash briefly blinded Gambo. The man didn't stop his lecture even as he stroked the boy's neck with the blade.

"You're certainly not afraid, are you? You were not afraid to run, even after you were told not to. So what are you afraid of?"

Gambo noticed that the boy's trousers were darkening around his groin.

"Look at you." The amir was unsympathetic. "What's this? You are afraid, after all." He threw his head back and laughed—a sound that reminded Gambo of a crow.

The women in their forced semicircle around this spectacle looked down at their feet. They didn't want to witness what they knew was about to happen.

The boy did not scream.

His head bounced twice and then rolled slowly toward the gathered crowd. A thin river of blood trickled in the same direction, snaking into the cracks of the dry earth. Muffled sobs convulsed the crowd. Everyone bowed down, not wanting to look, fearing they might catch the eye of the commander or one of his lieutenants.

The amir laughed, looked around, and ordered two women to take the boy's body away. Bodies were taken deeper into the forest, to a pit everyone avoided. Stories of unsettled spirits and headless bodies were whispered throughout the camps. How could any soul find peace when life was taken with such violence? If fear is the last thing you feel before death, how can you find eternal rest?

Gambo looked up briefly and thought she saw her mother directly across from her. She wanted to run over, to yell out, but she thought better of it. "Do nothing to draw attention to yourself." Another piece of advice from Ifeoma about how to survive the forest. Instead, Gambo held her hand up to her chest as a greeting, a way to tell her not to worry, but the woman did not respond. Gambo looked again and realized it was not Hajera at all, and then she started wondering where her mother and siblings were. Ifeoma had told her that she thought they were being held not far away, in an abandoned building where older women and their young children were often taken. Gambo had been hoping to run into them when she went to fetch water or food, but it was hard to shake the uneasy feeling that they had simply disappeared.

The next day, Gambo was told she would be marrying a Boko Haram soldier who had won the privilege of her hand by allegedly killing a dozen government forces in a fierce battle the week before. He was on his way back, she was told, from another village the group had targeted.

Gambo did not think. She just started running. She didn't know where she was going. All she knew was that she didn't want to marry a fighter and had to get out of the forest.

She had not even reached the body pit when she felt a hard object strike the back of her head. Two guards had been sent to retrieve her, and they were now dragging her back to the camp. They threw her to the ground by the baobab tree and took turns with the lashes. She stopped counting at twenty.

That night, she didn't sleep. She couldn't lie on her back or her side or her front; pain coursed through every inch of her body. It felt as if someone were ripping off her skin. Moving even the slightest bit was torture. The fabric of her mayafi was as sharp as a knife against her wounds. She worked hard to stifle the screams that rose inside her, to blink back the hot tears that welled in her eyes. Why was this happening to her? How could Allah create humans who were capable of such cruelty? Why wasn't he hearing her?

Gambo would soon learn that there was no limit to the cruelty one person could inflict on another. And also no limit to the stoicism of the one on the receiving end. Two days after her flogging, still burning with pain, she was "married" to Mohammad. And then she had no choice but to lie on her back while he made the marriage official. Pain surged through her, striking most deeply in the heart. Something was dying inside of her as she lay with her eyes open, staring up at nothing. She wished she could disappear from this world, wished she could stop feeling.

Eventually, she would.

ASMA'U

Asma'u could hear screaming. Her hand was bleeding, dark red. Then she realized that the screaming was coming from some-where inside of her. Her mother had fallen to the ground, and Asma'u was kneeling over her, tears and blood staining Hauwa's colourful wrapper. The man who had used the knife to separate them picked Asma'u up by her armpits. She kicked madly, cry-ing, arms struggling to get free. Blood sprayed everywhere.

"Mama!" Zainab and Musa had thrown themselves at their mother, clinging to her, wailing.

The man dragged Asma'u away from her siblings and took her deeper into the forest, where there was a camp. He threw her down on the ground and barked at someone to take a look at her wound. A woman fully covered in a dark mayafi appeared and took Asma'u's shaking hand in hers. Blood was still oozing, but it had also congealed all the way up to her elbow, and it was now black in some places. Flies and mosquitoes buzzed around them; the woman swatted them away.

"Don't cry," she whispered. "We'll clean you up."

The woman took a piece of fabric, which Asma'u recognized as part of a wrapper, dipped it in water, and washed her arm first, rubbing the dried blood from her elbow and then cleaning down to the open wound on the back of her right hand. Asma'u winced when the cloth made contact with her raw flesh. "Shhhh. Don't worry," the woman said. "This will heal. It's not a very deep cut."

After she had cleaned Asma'u's arm and hand, she took the piece of cloth and ripped it in two. She tied one half around Asma'u's wrist. "There. Try not to move it too much. It will stop bleeding soon. Come, child."

She took the young girl's hand and led her to a building that looked like an abandoned schoolroom divided into two. When they stepped inside, Asma'u could see that it was the sleeping quarters for women at the camp. There were people spread out across the floor. Most of them looked to be about Hauwa's age. What was this building? What had it been?

"Where are we?" Asma'u's voice was barely a whisper.

"You will stay with us tonight," the woman told her. "I can't promise you they won't take you tomorrow."

Asma'u shuddered. "Where would they take me?"

The woman's lips tightened into a line. "Please, child, you need to rest. Come." She led Asma'u to a spot on the cement floor. "Here. Rest your head tonight. Try to close your eyes for a little bit. Your mother will be okay. They don't kill older women unless they try to escape."

Asma'u sat in the spot she was directed to, but it all felt uneasy and awkward. She had never felt more frightened in her life. She wanted to ask the older woman a lot more. "Where is my family? Where are we? How do we get out?" But she somehow knew there were no answers to these questions. At least not tonight. Instead, she looked the woman in the eye and said, "*Nagode*. Thank you."

Asma'u was determined not to get married. *I don't want to marry anyone!* she screamed inside her head. A tight fear had gripped her heart all night, keeping her from getting any sleep. She was dreading the morning, and what the day might bring. She remembered what one of the men had said to her mother as they were being separated: "This girl is no longer yours. She now belongs to Baba Shekau." Those words fuelled her nightmares and she agonized over their meaning. Would they really bring her to Shekau, the feared leader of Boko Haram? Would they force her to marry a fighter? What if she refused? Would they strap a bomb to her and blow her up?

The next morning—her first in the forest—she and several other girls who had arrived the day before were taken to a small clearing under several trees. They had been forced to change from their colourful wrappers into dark mayafis. The girls, maybe a dozen of them, stood closely together, wondering what awaited them. Soon, an older man wearing a faded kameez approached the group with what looked like a small chalkboard.

"Sit down," he ordered, and the girls sat on the warm ground. The day had barely begun, but the temperature was already rising. The trees offered little relief from the heat of the morning sun. "I am your imam," the man said. "And this is our mosque. I will be teaching you your Islamic studies."

He stood in front of them and set down the chalkboard. Asma'u could read the one thing written on it: *Muhammad Yusuf*.

He then started yelling at the group. "You are all infidels! Non-believers. Destined for Jahannama. That's why you are here. We will teach you what it truly means to be a Muslim and then you can go to Jannat. You must start by forgetting everything you have learned in your *gwamnati* schools." He spat out the word for "government" as if it left a bad taste in his mouth.

The girls sat there for what felt like hours, listening to the imam as sweat beaded on their foreheads and ran down their necks. Asma'u closed her eyes and tried to pretend she was in her real school back at home, listening to a crazy teacher spouting crazy things. She didn't want or need to learn Islam. Although her family was not strictly religious, Friday prayers had been part of her life since she could remember. Why was this man telling them that they would all go to hell if they didn't listen and do as he ordered?

The imam then started quoting from Muhammad Yusuf, whom he called "our martyred founder." He said, "What will make you a soldier of Allah first and foremost, you make a complete disavowal of every form of unbelief: the government, worshipping tombs, idols, whatever. You come to reject it in your speech and your body and your heart. Moreover, Allah and His Messenger and the believers, you must love them in your speech, in your body, and in your heart."[5]

If he was speaking the truth, it seemed to Asma'u that they had all been living a life of iniquity. Schools were *haram*, the government was evil, Western teachings were corrupt, and any Muslim who did not accept these ideas was an infidel. Destined for the eternal inferno. Sitting in the heat of the afternoon sun, Asma'u felt like she was already there.

At the end of the day, an armed man she did not recognize joined the group and took over from the imam.

"Now that you are being cleansed in spirit, you will be ready to marry," he began. "We have chosen some nice husbands for you. They are brave fighters for our nation. But you will need to be good wives. Do you know how to be a good wife? Good wives take care of their husbands. They make sure their husbands have good suppers when they come home from battle. Good wives help the cause by bringing a new generation of fighters." He laughed, and the imam joined in.

"I don't want to get married." A girl's loud voice pierced the tension. Asma'u thought it might have been hers, since those words were running through her mind too. But it was a girl who had been sitting behind her all day and was now wailing in a full outburst. The others started nodding in agreement. Asma'u's head also bobbed and shook. No, she didn't want to marry either. Soon, the girls were in full revolt, with some of them standing up and threatening to run away. Three gunshots silenced them all. Asma'u ducked and looked around, but the man had fired into the air.

"You little fools! Listen to me, and listen closely. Do you think we are joking? This time, you got lucky. Consider it a warning. If you don't agree to marry, we will kill you. We will shoot you or cut your throats. Or we will put a bomb on you and send you back to your village, then blow you up and kill many others as well. What would you prefer? Would it be so horrible to be married to a nice boy?"

Asma'u could no longer suppress the sobs that were racking her chest. She started to cry, her small frame shaking uncontrollably. "I can't get married," she said over and over. "I'm only a child." This was not how she had imagined marriage—not at the age of twelve. Marriage wasn't supposed to be forced on you. "Don't kill us," she wailed. "We are just girls. Why would you kill us? We don't want to die."

The imam was surprisingly gentle in his response. "It is not so bad. If you do not marry, it will be worse for you. Just do what he tells you to do. I would advise you to marry, and then it won't be so hard."

Spent from the heat, the religious instruction, and the threat of marriage, the girls allowed themselves to be led back to the camp, where they were assigned to tents. Asma'u collapsed before she realized she'd had nothing to eat all day. A woman reached over and put a piece of *tuwo* in front of her. She stared at it for a long time, as if she had forgotten what it was, then she pinched small pieces of the gummy rice ball and put them in her mouth. It reminded her too much of home, of Hauwa's pepper soup, which is what she would have dipped the *tuwo* in. The thought of it was a trigger, a reminder of what she had already lost, a memory that hurt too much. She set the white ball down—she was too exhausted to be hungry anyway—and then laid her head on a straw mat and cried herself to a fitful, dreamless sleep.

Asma'u met Mohammadu the next day. She was certainly too young to be a wife, and he wasn't sure he wanted one. He was also young, a rising star within the ranks. He suspected his commanders wanted him to have a wife to tie him down, clip his wings a bit, keep his cockiness in check.

There was a brief wedding ceremony. The imam said a few words, and then she was suddenly a wife. Before moving on to marry another girl to another fighter, the imam had looked at her kindly, almost pityingly. Then Mohammadu led her away to his tent. She had no belongings with her—not even her wrapper, which she was sure had already been cut into rags.

Once inside, Mohammadu pushed her onto a straw mat. "Let's make this official." His voice was indifferent, and without any warning, he dropped his dirty pants and suffocated her with his body.

Asma'u had never felt such pain in her life. Her sister Binta had told her that she would start to bleed soon—it was part of growing up and becoming a woman. But Binta had never said that the bleeding would happen because a man tore her open. Hot tears flowed down her cheeks.

When it was over, he hiked up his pants and slapped her face.

"Why are you crying? Don't you understand how lucky you are? You little snivelling fool. I'll see you for supper. And you better be a good cook!" He laughed as if it were a big joke, then walked out of the tent.

Asma'u was shattered. She didn't move for a very long time. She thought it would be better if the ground swallowed her, better than having to be a wife to Mohammadu. How could she live here with this man she didn't even know? This stranger who had shattered her into shards of herself that she didn't recognize. She lay on her back, staring at the ceiling of the tent. Mosquitoes buzzed around, drawn to her by the scent of blood. She felt a pain in her hand and a warm trickle down her thumb. She had forgotten about the knife wound from the first day. The struggle with Mohammadu had opened the gash anew.

Asma'u held her hand up to her face and examined the cut. Dark blood was oozing out now, a red stream against the black scabs that had formed over it. She poked it with her left index finger, and more blood dripped down. She turned her head to her left and then her right. For the first time, she noticed the space itself. It was sparse. There was no bed, just the straw mat on which she had been violated. There was nothing nearby she could use to clean her hand. When she sat up, a pain immediately coursed from her abdomen to her pelvic bone. Wincing, she reached for the small piece of cloth that had been wrapped around the cut. It was stiff with dried blood now. Asma'u flattened it with the palm of her left hand and, using her teeth, bound the wound again. Strangely, she didn't feel as much pain in her hand as she did down below. Afraid to look, she shuffled herself to the edge of the mat. The wetness underneath her mayafi betrayed the reddish stain that had seeped into the straw. She held her stomach, gagging, and then threw up mostly bile on the floor. Her stomach was empty, but any hunger pangs were overwhelmed by the sharp pain in her lower body.

A silent prayer came into her head.

Subhanalillahi. Please, God, save me from these pains.

Food was a more immediate concern. Mohammadu would need supper in the evening, and Asma'u had never really cooked before. Her mind suddenly flashed back to the millet pudding she'd made when her mother was in a catatonic state after Binta and her father had been taken away. But Asma'u didn't know if there was millet here in the forest. Was there a space outside to make a fire? Where was the water? Gingerly, she stood up, but as soon as she was on her feet, her tiny frame convulsed with pain and she collapsed to the ground again. Her cheeks grew wet with tears, and she buried her head into her hands.

Subhanalillahi. Please, God, save me from these pains.

When Asma'u opened her eyes, she panicked. She didn't know how long she had slept or what time it was. She was sweating, though, so it still had to be daytime. She pulled herself up, cringing as she tried to stand again. She managed to stagger out of the tent. The pain between her legs was almost unbearable. But she knew she had to find food before Mohammadu returned.

Looking around, she saw that the camp was made up of other tents and a few abandoned buildings, one of which was the one she'd spent the night in when the older woman had cleaned her hand. She smelled a fire coming from somewhere and took a step toward the building. The fire was coming from behind it. As she took a few more tentative steps forward, two women appeared. One was the woman who had wrapped her hand.

"Child! Poor child. This is the one they gave to Mohammadu." She nodded gravely to the other woman, who looked down and shook her head. "What's your name, child?"

"Asma'u."

"Asma'u, I am Habibah. This is Amina."

Asma'u nodded. "I am looking for food. He says I need to cook."

"They're gone tonight." Habibah reached for Asma'u's hand. "Let's see. Oof! It reopened. Is it painful?"

Asma'u bit her lip in a feeble attempt to break the wall of tears that threatened to pour out of her. Habibah squeezed her arm gently, and that was all the permission she needed to let it go. The two older women exchanged looks. Amina's eyes filled up as she shook her head gently. The women each put a hand on one of Asma'u's shoulders and allowed her release.

"At least they are gone for the night. You can come and stay with us."

Asma'u was confused. Through tears, she told them she needed to fix some food for Mohammadu.

"No." Amina's voice was low and gentle. "The men have gone for the night. They went to take another village. Tonight, you can stay here with us."

The women led Asma'u back to the room where she had slept the first night. They brought her some *kuka*, soup made from dried baobab leaves, and then Habibah re-dressed her wound. This time, she rubbed a tonic on it. "It's from the baobab," she explained, and Asma'u didn't ask anything more. The baobab tree has mystical healing qualities and is a legendary, beloved part of the savannah. The leaves are boiled and eaten, and the fruit is believed to be life-sustaining. Asma'u had grown up with stories about the magic of the tree and how it saved animals, sheltered children, and fed whole communities.

Habibah had washed the bloody rag from the first night and was now tying a clean piece around Asma'u's hand. From the women, Asma'u learned that when she collapsed after being wrenched from her mother, the amir's men took her deeper into the forest. She wondered aloud where Binta was and asked Habibah if she had seen anyone who looked like her, just a little older, and had arrived in the forest a week or so earlier. The women shook their heads. So many girls come and go, they said. They're here one day and gone the next, taken deeper into the forest. It's possible Binta had been married off to a commander. That would be for the best.

"Why?" Asma'u couldn't imagine there was anything good about being married to a Boko Haram fighter.

"You'll see," Amina told her.

She learned where the communal kitchen was, and although Mohammadu expected her to prepare his meals herself, she was relieved to find out that the older women did most of the cooking in this camp and she would be able to rely on them for some of the meals. The women told her that her husband was a young fighter who showed much promise, and that if he wasn't killed by government forces, he would be promoted to commander one day. When that happened, they said, Asma'u would possibly move with him to another camp, deeper in the forest. She would have more help to cook and clean, and they might even graduate from a tent to a hut. "But," Habibah cautioned, "he will take another wife, maybe a third, and then you'll have to fight for your place in the order."

Asma'u felt dizzy. She was still struggling with the pain between her legs and was relieved that she wouldn't have to spend the night back in the tent with Mohammadu. But she was apprehensive about what the future held if she didn't try to escape.

Habibah seemed to read her mind. "I know what you are thinking. I would tell you not to try just yet. There are those who have made it out. But if they catch you . . ." She shook her head.

"They said they would kill us," Asma'u said.

Habibah nodded.

"Have you seen them kill people?"

Amina ran a finger across the width of her neck. Asma'u decided that was something she didn't want to see. Or experience.

"There are ways to get out," Habibah told her. "You'll find out everything in time."

Asma'u wanted to know why the two of them had not tried to escape.

"Oh, believe me, we did." Amina lifted Habibah's mayafi to reveal her scarred back. At least a dozen raised crimson marks, the punishment for trying to leave the forest.

"I was lucky I wasn't killed," Habibah said. "The amir wasn't here that day, so I was spared. But they have killed many others. We have both seen it."

They went on to talk about young girls who were caught trying to escape. They were killed by the husbands they were trying to run away from. Some were mercifully shot in the head. Others were beheaded. The stories made Asma'u wonder whether she'd be better off dead than married to a man she didn't know or like.

"Opportunities will come," Habibah said. "But you must know the way, or you will end up deep in the forest and it will be impossible to leave." Stories abounded of girls who got lost and wandered into another camp run by an amir who was even more brutal and violent than the one they'd escaped.

The women explained that the best time to get free was when the military raided the forest to try to dislodge the fighters and break up the camps. There was often chaos in these moments. The guards were too busy running for their own lives to chase down anyone trying to flee. "When the bombs fall, that's the time to run."

Asma'u wondered if the bombs ever killed the wrong people. People like them.

"Of course," Habibah told her. "Sometimes it's just unlucky."

How much unluckier could you be than to get killed by government forces who were supposed to be rescuing you from captivity?

Once again, Habibah seemed to read her mind. "Try to get some rest, child. Tomorrow will come soon."

Mohammadu returned the following afternoon, having razed a village close to Maiduguri with his men. Their trucks were loaded with food and other stolen items: generators, gas, even a few boxes of bottled water. They talked loudly, boasting of their achievements—the people they'd killed, the houses they'd pillaged. They laughed loudly, bits of chewed khat flying out of their mouths. Asma'u was bringing soup and *tuwo* in for supper when Mohammadu came to the tent.

He took one sip of the soup and flung the bowl on the ground. "This is disgusting!"

His voice was menacing as he took a step toward her. Before Asma'u could even process what he'd said, she fell backwards as his fist struck the side of her head. She put her arms up to protect herself from the blows. He started yelling.

"How do you expect me to eat that shit?" he screamed. "Don't you know how to make soup? You useless little bitch."

"I'm sorry, I'm sorry," she whispered. "Don Allah. Please." She was on the ground, cowering in front of him, heart beating with a fear that was new to her. He could kill her right here and that would be the end of it. Her family would never find her.

He started kicking her, in the stomach first and then in the back. "Stop your crying, you little bitch. Grow up." He kicked the overturned bowl toward her and then walked out of the tent.

Asma'u started to shake. Her whole body trembled, and with each shudder, she felt pain. Pain in her side, in her head, and between her legs. She was too tired to cry, too despondent to care.

Mohammadu came back later that night, breath sour from khat, eyes bloodshot, the effect of a pill all the men took before they went into a fight. Asma'u felt he was possessed by something otherworldly as he pushed her down onto the mat and ripped her open again and again. Her eyes were wide, fixated on the tarpaulin above her. She felt completely outside of herself. When he was finally finished, he rolled over and began to snore. It sounded like thunder. She curled herself into a ball and prayed.

Subhanalillahi. Please, God, save me from these pains.

The beatings never stopped. In fact, they got worse when Mohammadu started using a whip made of some kind of animal hide. It wasn't just the food he had an issue with. It was everything.

"You refused my proposal at first." The whip landed on her back.

"This house is a mess. Don't you know how to clean?" The whip landed on her shoulder.

"Look at this. These pants are still dirty. Have you never washed clothes before?" The whip landed across her chest. Her legs. Her face. Her head.

In his estimation, his child bride could do nothing right, and worse, she was not falling pregnant. He was expected to help produce the next generation of Boko Haram fighters. Many of his friends were already complaining about the babies that kept them awake at night. What he didn't know was that his wife had not started menstruating yet.

"Why are you not yet with child?" he would bellow. And then he would put more force into her, willing something to happen that wasn't yet physically possible.

For Asma'u, relief came only when he was on another mission, attacking another village, but she was slowly fading away from herself. She even stopped staying with Habibah and Amina on the nights when Mohammadu was away, preferring to be alone in the tent.

On those days and nights, she would sit on the straw mat, still stained with her blood and her tears, and think about her family. Where were her siblings and her mother? Where was her father? Maybe Binta had escaped. Would they have run for freedom during a government raid? What if they were killed by a bomb that was supposed to save them?

Subhanalillahi. Don Allah, save me from this pain. End this suffering for me. Make my family whole again.

4
ZARA, 2016 & 2017

ZARA IMAGINED HER eldest brother, Abdulkadiri, hovering over her schoolwork, trying to pinpoint where she'd made the mistake that led to the wrong answer on her math test. It was a long equation, and his brow would have furrowed as he traced the tip of his pencil over each of her calculations. *He was so smart*, she thought. He had graduated from university in Mubi and later studied in the country's capital, Abuja. He'd joined the military and headed to Lagos to begin his service.

It was just after prayers, one morning in 2016, and she remembered how Abdulkadiri used to make sure his younger siblings were prepared for their school day. Zara lived with their sister, Salamatu, and her husband, but Abdulkadiri used to check in on her every day to make sure she was doing her schoolwork. After all, he was the one who'd paid her fees; he'd wanted to make sure he got a return on his investment.

He knew Zara was a good student. From grades one to four, she was more interested in playing games with her friends than learning math or English, but she still managed to finish first in her class. It wasn't until the fifth grade, when she dropped a few spots, that she realized she had to work to maintain her standing. If she or any of her siblings did well on an exam, Abdulkadiri would slaughter a chicken for them—a special celebration feast. The slightly charred sweet taste of a chicken cooked over the fire was incentive for them all. Chickens ran all over the village, but they were saved for special occasions or sold for a handsome sum to those who could afford them. There would be no chicken tonight for Zara's latest math exam.

"I hate math," she would always complain to him.

And his response would be the same every time: "How are you going to be a doctor if you don't know how much medicine to measure out?"

Zara would sigh and pull her long blue uniform dress over her head. She would gather her notebooks and give her brother a hug before skipping out the door with a wave. He would always smile and wave back. She often wondered how they could be related. He was fair; she was dark. He was tall; she was short. He was great at math; she struggled to understand it.

Isa, their father, had championed education with all eleven of his children, drilling into them the importance of learning. Not finishing high school was not an option. His own father—a traditionalist who was suspicious of the missionary schools that were springing up in different communities at that time—didn't allow Isa and his siblings to be educated. White people's schools would corrupt their way of life, he said.

But Isa saw things differently. "You must learn to read and write," he told his own children. "Even if you don't end up working in the city, you'll be able to help me and your mother, and all your aunts and uncles, write letters and read documents. Look at us. We never learned, you see. We never had the opportunity that you do, so you must take advantage of it."

Isa was a bricklayer, and the work was hard on his back, his body. "It is better to be able to use your mind," he would tell his children, "so that you can save your body." A lifetime of manual labour had left him in constant pain, and these days he was mostly focused on farming guinea corn, or sorghum, thanks to a program offered by an NGO. Farming wasn't that much easier on his body, but he preferred using his calloused fingers to tend to the long stalks that grew miraculously out of the cracked soil. Sometimes, Zara would join him after school, checking the plants carefully, turning over the leaves to inspect their undersides, studying the stalks to make sure there were no parasites.

As she made her way down the road from her sister's home, Zara could see her school in the distance. It was in better shape these days, thanks to a facelift and a new roof. She had spent much of her student career staring at the cream paint peeling from the walls or through the cracks in the building's broken windows. When it was too hot to be indoors, classes moved outside, and the students sat in the shade of trees.

She was already looking forward to class break, when she and her friends would gather at the back of the school and play their chanting game, dancing and taking turns falling into and bouncing up from the net of hands the group made. It was the best part of her day.

Entering the schoolyard, she saw one of her teachers through an open window, preparing the day's English lesson. It was Zara's favourite subject, and the one in which she excelled. She dreamed of attending university abroad someday. She was just finishing her second year of junior secondary school, the equivalent to grade eight. One more year here and three at senior secondary school, and then it would be time for university.

Abdulkadiri used to promise her that he would support her if she could gain admission to a foreign university. She knew how important it was to finish school. She'd heard that girls who marry at an early age are most at risk of dying in childbirth. Zara did not want to be a statistic, and she didn't want to let her father down. He kept reminding her that school was her only way out of Duhu, their small village in Borno State. "Look at me," he would say. "Do you want to be a farmer for the rest of your life?"

Zara's mother, Zainabu, was also illiterate. She had been raised by one of her aunts after her parents died when she was only three. The aunt sent her own children to school but kept Zainabu at home to do housework. She married Zara's father at the age of fifteen and gave birth to Abdulkadiri shortly after that, and then to ten more babies in the years following. A few months shy of fourteen, Zara was not so much younger than her mother had been when she had her first child. The thought gave her pause. Zara could not imagine being a mother.

More than a year before Zara was taken into the forest, the course of her life had already shifted. It was a hot morning, early, when the phone rang, and she heard her father answer with a friendly "*Sannu!* Hello!" The caller was a former neighbour who now lived in Lagos. For Isa, it was always a welcome event to hear from an old friend. Zara listened expectantly for news from the south. She watched her father and then saw his face pale. She heard an anguished sound escape from his throat, and his face crumpled. Her heart started to beat very fast, faster than she thought possible. Isa was shaking his head and saying, "No, no, no. Abdulkadiri. No, there must be a mistake. It's not possible. It cannot be true. He is coming home for a visit soon. We just spoke to him the other day."

The friend kept apologizing to Isa, but there would never be enough apologies for this tragedy. Their beloved son was dead. Murdered. The friend had heard the news from the military.

"May God have mercy. I saw your son just last week. He was in good spirits. May God have mercy on his soul," he repeated. "I'm so sorry."

Isa fell to his knees. Zainabu started to wail, collapsing next to his feet. Her cries came from somewhere deep inside, somewhere Zara did not recognize and did not wish to know. Their son, Zara's beloved brother Abdulkadiri, was gone. What would Zara do without him? Who would help her study for her math exams? Who would slaughter a chicken for her? Who would pay her school fees?

Abdulkadiri had always embraced the responsibility that came with being the firstborn. He saw it as his duty to help his parents, who worked tirelessly to provide for their large family. He was fifteen when Zara was born, and he doted on her as if she were a little doll. As she got older, he took on a more active role in her studies, recognizing her natural gifts with language and problem-solving. He became convinced she would be the first doctor in their family—math be damned.

His siblings, especially his sisters, adored him. As laughing brother and exacting guardian, he filled the void left in their lives by parents who were constantly labouring and were unschooled. Isa and Zainabu relied on him to help them read and write letters and translate the written word into their illiterate lives. He had graduated senior school at the top of his class and gone on to university studies in Mubi and later in Abuja. When he told his family he had decided to join the military, they were confused, but he was adamant that he wanted to serve the country, and that enlisting was how he could make a difference.

He had been posted to Lagos as a brilliant and talented new recruit. He called home often, talking to his siblings, checking in, making sure the younger ones were keeping up with their schoolwork and the older ones were helping their parents with the chores he'd left behind. Just the other day, Abdulkadiri had called home with the news of a promotion and a promise to come back to see his family in the coming weeks.

The details of his death were unclear. He had been arguing with another recruit, a soldier who his friends said was envious of Abdulkadiri's recent promotion. The argument became heated, and the other recruit shot him with his army-issued rifle and then ran, deserting his unit altogether. The military was still looking for him, and the family was assured he would be punished for his crime. But a beloved son, an admired brother, and a promising young soldier lay dead.

"No, it's not possible!" Zara ran outside and buried her head in her hands, covering herself in denial. How could this be true? It could not. Her brother was only twenty-eight years old. He was her protector, her teacher, her ticket to a higher education and a life beyond their village. How could he be gone just like that? It couldn't be true. Maybe it was another soldier who was killed.

Zara went back inside and called her sister.

"I just talked to him two days ago," Salamatu said, her voice flat. Their father had already broken the news to her, and she'd half expected Zara's call.

"It can't be true," Zara pleaded. "Tell me it's not true."

Salamatu said she would find out and call back. But when the phone rang again, Zara already knew.

"It's true, little sister. Our brother has left us too soon." Her voice was low, like a whisper. Salamatu did not want Zara to know she was crying.

Abdulkadiri had set an example for all ten of his younger siblings, demonstrating that hard work and determination could lift them all from their circumstances. He showed them that by the way he lived and the decisions he made. When he moved to Lagos to serve the country, it gave them all something to aspire to; it made anything seem possible.

For Zara, the loss was immeasurable. She had been working hard at school to make him proud, to show him that she deserved his support and encouragement. Now that the one person who'd promised to lift her out of this place was gone, what motivation was left? Who would support her now that her brother was dead?

=====

2017

She heard voices all around her. "This girl does not believe she is pregnant. Someone has to tell her. Her blood pressure is very high. We have to do something about it."

Zara opened her eyes. Where was she? She sat up and looked around. She was at a hospital. Her aunt was talking to a doctor, gesturing broadly with her hands as both of them glanced over at Zara's bed. The last thing she remembered was one of the nurses asking her how old she was. And then they did some tests, poking and prodding. She felt like she was out of her body, looking down on herself. She had closed her eyes to try to shut it all out.

But now it all came back to her in a rush of disbelief, in pangs of grief for a life lost. Her life. Her old life. She was pregnant. She didn't want to be pregnant. She wouldn't believe she was pregnant.

I'm just a child still. How can I be having a baby? I still have to finish school.

She could hear the nurses and her aunt and the doctor debating whether to tell her.

"She needs to know. But her blood pressure is too high. It will upset her. Still, we need to tell her. She is just a child. She will be having a child. We must tell her."

Zara already knew. It was confirmation of what her aunt and others had suspected for the past few weeks, ever since she'd returned from the forest. By the time her aunt and the doctor reached her bedside, she was already sobbing uncontrollably, shaking her head, unable to speak. She wanted to go back inside her head, back to where Abdulkadiri was still alive and helping her with her math homework, back to her school with the paint peeling from the walls, back to the playground with her friends.

At her aunt's house in Yola, she sat stone-faced. Her relief at having escaped the forest was now overshadowed by the sinking knowledge that her life had been irrevocably altered. She put a hand on her stomach as if to try to stop it from growing. What if she could get rid of it before it grew? There were doctors who could help with that—Zara had heard of other girls having abortions. But she also knew that almost all those stories ended with the deaths of the mothers, and Zara did not want to die.

Zara's aunt was on the phone to her parents back in Duhu. Her relief at hearing their voices was quickly tempered by an anxiety that was also growing inside her. She couldn't imagine what they were thinking. The future her father had worked so hard to secure for her, to construct for her, now seemed in ruins. Could she even go home? Or would she bring shame on her family by returning with a Boko Haram baby?

She remembered the horror she was greeted with when she first stumbled out of the forest. She had been walking for days—she didn't know how many—and hunger and thirst were making her hallucinate. She thought she saw some houses in the distance and some people gathered under a tree. But she wasn't sure if her eyes were playing tricks on her.

She called out. "*Sannu!*"

Were they real, or was it all a mirage? She called out again and realized they were real, but the villagers started walking away as she approached. She would never forget the fear and suspicion in their eyes.

She could hear them in the distance: "A Boko Haram spy! Maybe a Boko Haram wife!"

Zara shook her head no, waved her arms. "*Taimake ni!* Help me! *Don Allah, taimake ni!* Please help me!" she implored. "I am not with them. I ran away from the forest."

The villagers continued to move away from her, talking among themselves, debating whether she was an emissary or an escapee of the terror group.

"Please," she begged. "Please help me. I was in the forest, but I ran away. See? I am all alone. I have nothing on me, nothing with me. Please stop." She started to cry.

The villagers finally stopped and looked at her, taking in her small bedraggled frame, tattered clothing, and dirt-caked feet.

"She looks terrible," one of the women said.

"She looks like a schoolgirl. Maybe she's from Chibok?" suggested another.

"Come, child." An older woman with a kind face held out her hand, motioning to Zara. "Come with us. You'll be safe here."

In the village, she continued to get strange looks from passersby. Somewhat sheltered now by the people who took her in, she kept her gaze at her feet, afraid to make eye contact with anyone else but grateful she was finally able to stop walking. She couldn't even guess how long she'd been on the road.

"Sit down here," said the woman with the kind eyes. She shook out a straw mat and laid it on the ground, motioning for Zara to have a seat. The women gave her some *tuwo* with soup, and she ate hungrily. She hadn't eaten since she'd left the forest days ago. She had taken nothing with her. There had been nothing to take. She wondered if anyone had gone looking for her the morning after she left.

She had come up with her plan to leave because he was away. He was out in the bush with the others, on a mission, probably attacking another village and taking more hostages. He often went out on missions and would sometimes stay away for several nights. She was never sure how long he'd be gone. She never asked.

"I am just going out to do my business," she was ready to tell the guards if they stopped her. "I need to relieve myself." But fortune was with her on this night: the guard stationed in front of her hut was asleep. She took one step away. And then another. And another. Once she was in the bush, she just kept walking. Slowly at first, so as not to make too much noise with her feet in the leaves and grass. She kept looking behind to see if anyone was following. She saw no one, so she kept walking, one foot in front of the other. As she moved farther from the encampment, she took a deep breath and held it. She didn't know where she was going or which direction she should be headed. She just kept walking. Finally, after she was confident she hadn't been followed, she broke into a run.

The darkness enveloped her. It was easier to breathe in the cooler air of the night. She wasn't sure how long she ran, but she zigzagged one way and then the other, just in case they had set off after her. As soon as she felt certain that no one had followed her, she slowed to catch her breath.

It was still very dark, and she had no idea where she was or where she was going. All that mattered was that she was leaving the forest. She would find a way back to her sister's house, back to her family, back to school and everything she had been taken from. Exhausted, she sat down against a tree, pulled her headscarf over her head, and closed her eyes, shrinking into the earth, hoping it would swallow her. When she opened her eyes again, it was light. She stood up and surveyed her surroundings. She was still deep in the forest, with no option but to start walking and hope that civilization was not too far away.

Don Allah, ka taimake ni ka taimake ni na tsira. Please, God, help me to survive this. Please, God, guide my way.

She prayed silently at first and then out loud, her prayers echoing through the dense bush.

But after four days—or was it five?—with no food or water and no clarity of direction, a small twinge of panic started to replace the hunger in her stomach. What if she ran into another group of Boko Haram militants? What if she died of hunger or thirst out here? What if they were looking for her? Had she covered her tracks well enough? She picked a leaf off a tamarind tree and stuffed it in her mouth. Bitter. She forced herself to swallow it anyway. She trudged on, silently asking God to let her see her parents one more time, dead or alive.

Don Allah, ka taimake ni ka taimake ni na tsira.

It was hot; the humidity drained much of her energy, and there were flying bugs swarming her head. She swatted at them as she pushed forward, being careful not to trip over branches and stumps. Her head started to hurt, and her throat was so parched that she could no longer even send her prayers out into the air. She was starting to see things in her path—hallucinations springing from exhaustion. Men with guns, but when she ran, they did not run after her. An animal—was it a goat?—darted through the trees in the distance, but when she went after it, it disappeared. Which way was she going? What if she had taken a bad turn and ended up back in the camp, where her Boko Haram husband was waiting to beat the life out of her?

And then she heard running water. Could it be real or was it another trick being played on her by a parched mind and depleted body? She came upon a river, narrow in width, but the water was indeed running—fresh water, warm to the touch but clean nonetheless. She scooped handfuls of it to her mouth, drinking in the life it held. She drank of the river until her stomach was full, then splashed it over her face. Looking around to make sure she was alone, she undressed and waded in, scrubbing her body with her hands, first gently and then vigorously, almost violently, as if to wash away everything that had happened to it in the last five months.

When she had finished in the river, Zara got dressed and continued walking. There appeared to be a clearing ahead. Were those houses? She picked up her pace, heart racing with hope that this journey, this walk, this nightmare she had been living through would perhaps finally be over. In the distance, she thought she saw several people sitting under a tree.

"*Taimake ni!* Help me!"

Weeks later, back in her parents' house in Duhu, the nightmare was in her belly. Her father had taken one look at her and knew right away that she was pregnant.

"There's a baby inside," Isa told her.

"No!" she cried. "How can I have a baby? I am still a child."

It was the same argument she'd made to the villagers who took her in. She stayed with them for a few weeks, and they cared for her as they would their own child. They gave her fresh clothes to replace the dirty torn dress and headscarf she had been wearing for days. They made a pudding of millet and gave her steaming bowls of it, telling her she needed to eat to help feed the child growing inside.

Zara did not speak the first few days. It was as if her pleas for help were the last words she wanted to speak out loud. The villagers seemed to understand and gave her the space they thought she needed. When they sensed that she was coming back to herself, they asked her where she was from. If her parents were alive, they said, they would no doubt want to collect her. Believing she was the only one taken, Zara told them she thought they were still alive. She told them the name of her village, and someone eventually got word to them. Shortly after, her aunt arrived from Yola to take over from the kind strangers.

Zara thought her father would be angry—all his plans for her, interrupted. She said she would have an abortion, despite her fears of dying from it. But Isa would not hear of it.

"It's illegal," he told her. "You will have the child, and your mother and I will help you care for him or her. You can then go back to school if you want to. But this is not your fault. We will love the baby. It doesn't matter."

The truth of the matter was that Zara's parents were just happy to have found her alive. They had all been separated when

Boko Haram came to their village. And her parents had spent five sleepless, anxious months wondering what had happened to her.

They remember the day differently from Zara. But all of them remember that rumours about the militants had circulated for days. They had overrun Gwoza and were on the march south to Gulak and Duhu. But then word came that the military had repelled them from Gulak, so people's concern dissipated and they continued on with their lives, trying to make themselves believe Boko Haram wouldn't come to Duhu.

That all changed one Friday afternoon. Zara was at her parents' home with her sister Salamatu, and they had just prepared the evening meal. She was about to call her two younger sisters and little brother for supper. They heard a commotion outside and saw soldiers running, yelling, "*Gudu! Gudu!*" Then there were people darting in every direction, and she knew it had to be Boko Haram even before she heard the cries of "Allahu Akbar!" and the gunshots piercing the din of daily life.

"Mama!" Salamatu's voice was shaking. "It is Boko Haram shooting. I remember this is how they came to Maiduguri." Salamatu was married in the capital of Borno State a few years earlier and had been there when the militants attacked the town. The military had been able to repel the attack, but Salamatu and her husband, Dauda, were badly shaken. They decided to move south to be closer to family in Duhu, where they thought Boko Haram would be less likely to attack.

Now it was time to run again.

"Mama, we should go."

Zainabu looked at her two older daughters and then at their father. Zara knew what no one wanted to say out loud: her father would not be able to run.

"Let's eat something first, and then we will go," Zainabu suggested.

But everyone was too frightened to be hungry.

Finally, Zara's father spoke up. "I will stay. My body will not allow me to follow you. You must leave tonight, when it's dark. Go to the hills and stay there. Hopefully the army will come soon and drive out the terrorists. I will stay here. It will be okay. Try not to worry."

The thought was incomprehensible to Zara. How could they leave her father here by himself?

"Papa, I will stay with you," she said.

Isa raised his hand to say no. "You must go. It will be all right."

"We will come back soon," promised Zainabu.

There was no time for long goodbyes. Zara, Salamatu, their mother, and the three youngest children fled in the dark, heading up the hills next to the village. They stayed there for four nights and five days, subsisting on the maize cakes and water they had brought with them. Other villagers also straggled up the hill, describing the horrors that Boko Haram had wrought on their town.

"The streets are littered with bodies, and bugs are feasting on them," one woman said as she passed Zara's family.

"Everything has been burned. There is no one left," another woman said. "Disease has infected the entire place. There is vomit and blood in the streets."

On the fifth night, the sisters could stand it no longer. Zara and Salamatu decided to go back to the house to see what had become of it, and of their father.

They agreed to split up to increase the odds that at least one of them would make it back. Salamatu would take a longer, more convoluted route, and Zara would head down the path they'd come up. They parted on a promise to meet at home, and with a squeeze of hands, the two young women set off on their separate journeys.

Zara's was short-lived. The militants had tracked the footsteps of the villagers and were lying in wait for others to come up the path. They had not expected anyone to come down. She turned when she saw them and tried to run in another direction, careful not to lead them to where her mother and her younger siblings were hiding, but they were too quick. She had barely turned around when she felt hands grab her from behind. She shuddered and then struggled to break loose, but she knew it was futile. She kicked and thrashed while being held, her arms twisted behind her back. She thought of her sister, thankful they had not travelled together, and said a quick prayer that Salamatu would make it home and find their father still alive.

The men kept her in the woods for four days and five nights. Her mouth was dry from thirst and she begged them for water incessantly, but they ignored her pleas. She would chew on leaves and grass, but they did little to staunch the growing growl of an empty stomach.

"Isn't it nicer to be with us than the army?" they said, taking turns taunting her. "Go ahead, wait for the army to come find you. Where are they?"

She refused to look them in the eye and shrugged her arm away whenever one tried to drag her through the woods to keep pace.

On the fifth day, they arrived at what looked like a camp. Zara could see ramshackle shelters made of branches and tarps. She could smell the smoke of a fire before she saw it. She heard a baby crying and the voice of a mother trying to quiet her. What was this? A village in the woods?

One of the men turned to look at her, a glint in his eye. "Welcome home."

She stayed in the camp for nearly five months. They told her constantly that she was getting married, laughing and joking about which one of them she would be better off with. She met other women who had already been assigned husbands and witnessed several other marriages during this time.

She lived in a rotting thatched hut with several other girls. New girls were always coming in, and others would leave to be married. The days revolved around the two hours they spent in religious studies sessions, under an umbrella tree on the other side of the encampment.

Zara was always thinking about escape, but the girls' hut was guarded closely at all times. It was the place where they kept future wives. She started to despair after several weeks. Had Salamatu made it home? Was their father still alive? Were her mother and younger siblings still hiding in the hills? She thought about school and how she was supposed be starting her last year of junior secondary, year nine, and then it would be time for the senior school and eventually university. She wondered if she would ever see any of it again.

In the fourth month of her captivity, she was summoned for marriage. It didn't matter that she was only thirteen, still a child. The militants brushed aside her protestations and gave her to a fighter, Khalid.* He seemed to be quite senior in the hierarchy and was always seen with the camp's amir, the head of the commune they lived in.

Zara moved into Khalid's house, or hut. It was slightly bigger than the one she'd shared with the other girls. Very quickly, she understood what her role was: to keep it clean, to cook all the meals, to stay silent, and not to cry when he lay with her in the dark.

Khalid would often go off with the amir and others to fight what he called the *kuffar*—the government, the military, and anyone who did not practise the strict Islam that Boko Haram demanded of its followers and its captives. The first time he left, he did not return for two nights. On the third day, Zara casually walked out of the hut with a plastic jug, to make it look like she was going to fetch water. She thought she had a clear path out of the camp, but a guard grabbed her from behind. Her heart felt like it had stopped, and the blood drained from her face.

"Where do you think you're going? The river is the other way." He struck her across the face and hauled her back to her

---

* This is not his real name. Zara refuses to speak his name, so we have decided to call him Khalid.

hut. Her husband was told on his return, and he reprimanded her by hitting her in the head with the butt end of his gun.

That blow stirred a defiance that had been simmering inside Zara for the past four months. She would not be slave or wife to this stranger, this killer. She would find a way to leave.

She tried to escape twice more, but both times she was caught by a vigilant guard who no doubt feared the wrath of Khalid if he returned to find his wife missing. Each time, the butt end of his AK-47 found her head. Each time, she wondered if he would finally make good on his threats to kill her.

She refused to meet Khalid's gaze and looked down every time he came into the hut. Most days he left her alone, more consumed with the work of terrorism than with terrorizing his wife. He and the amir would have long meetings about which village they would attack next and what they needed for the camp. Food was always a priority. Boko Haram was always worried about running out of food. In this way, Zara knew she was luckier than others. Because of Khalid's position, they were guaranteed certain provisions.

At night, she would often hear crying in the huts nearby, followed by the sound of beatings. New young girls were brought into the camp all the time. Those who were not chosen to be married to fighters went for training. Several were sent out of the camp with bombs strapped to their tiny frames. She'd heard that some of these girls were sent back to their own villages, to blow up what was left of their communities—their relatives, friends, family. She decided that if ever she was forced to strap a bomb to herself, she would blow herself up before arriving back home. She couldn't imagine killing herself, but she didn't want others to die.

To an outsider who didn't know how the women came to live in the forest, camp life would have looked strangely normal. There was a communal food store where rations of maize and millet were doled out on a semi-regular basis. Everyone attended daily classes on Islam, and in the evenings, small fires were lit all over camp as the wives of the fighters prepared their meals.

Zara kept mostly to herself. She did not talk to anyone but God. *Whatever happens, happens. I completely trust you to guide the path, wherever it might lead. But please let me see my family one more time. Alive or dead. Please let my family be alive, that I might meet them again, even if it is only for one last time.*

She prayed all day, and often all night. Sleep did not come easily in the forest. And it was at night when Zara's thoughts ran away from her, awakening the anxieties that daylight often kept at bay.

Near the end of her fifth month in the forest, she heard Khalid talking with the amir about going to Maiduguri. They would be gone at least two nights. She decided immediately that she would make another attempt to escape the first night. This time, she would wait until after dark. And instead of pretending to fetch water, she would tell the guards she had to relieve herself.

She looked up to the sky and said a silent prayer. *Don Allah, taimake ni. Taimake ni.*

And then out loud, as if to give her prayer a witness: "Dear God, please help me. Please help me."

Finally, she implored the one person she thought might be able to hear her: her brother Abdulkadiri.

It was perhaps a blessing that he had been killed a year before. He didn't have to see his little sister disappear into the forest and his home village get razed by terrorists. He didn't see his father's fields burned or his mother fall into a deep depression after Zara was taken. Those five long months took an immeasurable toll on the family. Abdulkadiri would have been angry. Zara wasn't quite sure what he would have done, but sometimes at night, when sleep eluded her, she imagined her brother in his army uniform, taking on Boko Haram by himself. She sometimes even pictured him killing Khalid, an image that gave her a degree of comfort on those long nights when she was still a captive wife in a dark forest.

When she was finally reunited with her family, the joy was short-lived. Her parents cried when Zara returned to her village. Her aunt had brought her from Yola, after all her medical checks were finished and she was sure that Zara was ready to rejoin her family. Her father, who had been pressuring his sister to bring her home, was overcome when she arrived.

"I didn't want to believe we would all be together again." Isa's face was wet. He openly wept seeing his daughter.

Her mother had no words. She just held Zara to her chest and kept looking at her, stroking her hair and her cheeks, as if to say, "Is it really you, daughter?"

Zara continued to live with her sister, Salamatu, and her husband, Dauda, throughout her pregnancy. It upset her to see her former schoolmates walking the well-worn path to her old school while she sat at home waiting for the baby to come. She started to wonder if she would ever go back to school, despite her parents' and sister's promises that they would look after the baby so she could finish her education.

She grew embarrassed and afraid to venture out. The first few times she'd wandered to the market, she noticed the long stares of neighbours. They seemed to be judging her, the young mother-to-be of a Boko Haram baby. She couldn't walk across the street without hearing a snicker or feeling eyes follow her. One time, someone spat at her and called her a Boko Haram wife.

Eventually, Salamatu stopped sending her out on errands, which she had initially hoped would help Zara reintegrate into village life. She noticed the silent condemnation her sister endured—as if she were responsible for her predicament—and it angered Salamatu. But there was no place to put that growing rage. She wanted to shout to the world that none of this was Zara's fault, that everyone should experience first-hand what her little sister had. Zara, on the other hand, looked and felt vacant most of the time. If she was angry or upset by what people said and did, her face betrayed nothing. She became ambivalent about her life and didn't want to think about caring for a baby, let alone giving birth.

Salamatu worried that her bright, beautiful sister had lost interest in everything, even as she was carrying new life in her body. Zara sat at home every day, helping with the cleaning and the cooking, but she was despondent, sleepwalking her way through the days. Salamatu made her favourite foods—fish soup, fire-cooked chicken and rice—but Zara never wanted to eat, even when her sister pleaded with her about the health of the baby.

Salamatu never asked her sister what had happened in the forest. Part of her didn't want to know, and part didn't want to pry. She wished she knew what to say when she caught Zara staring into space or heard her crying out in her sleep, haunted by the memories that came to her in the dark.

Dauda, Salamatu's husband, promised Zara that when her baby turned two, he would pay for her to go to a boarding school, and he and Salamatu and her parents would look after the baby until she graduated—even from university, if that was what she wanted. "It's what Abdulkadiri would have done," he told her. "And now that he is no longer here, it is my responsibility to make sure you finish school and live up to your potential."

Dauda was a police officer, and he worked long hours to support Salamatu, the couple's own young daughter, and Zara. He had an easy smile and an earnest manner, and he and Salamatu were a handsome young couple.

Zara had lived with them since she was five. It took some pressure off her parents, who still had to look after her younger sisters and brother. And now, with a baby coming, Zara felt safe and cared for in their home, even in her depression. It's what she needed after so many months in the forest: security and the promise of a future, despite the hard road that lay ahead. She knew, from observing her sister and her parents, that Duhu was not the easiest place to raise a child. But with the help of her family, she knew the child would be loved, just as she and her siblings were, and given every opportunity to grow up and have a normal life, regardless of how he or she came into being. When she saw how her family had accepted and was making plans for this child she'd never wanted, Zara began to think that perhaps even she might one day feel love. Maybe—*inshallah*—everything would be as it was meant to be.

5
RUNNING

ASMA'U

Asma'u could no longer remember how long she had been in the forest. She was attending Islamic lessons during the day and cooking or cleaning at other times, but mostly she was just trying to avoid the gaze of Mohammadu. Mercifully, he'd seemed to lose interest in her, but as long as he was around, the threat of a beating was always imminent. Thankfully, he was away more frequently as Boko Haram became bolder, targeting bigger cities in Borno and Adamawa. Earlier that year, they had also taken 276 Chibok schoolgirls into the forest, garnering an international reputation as one of the world's most feared terror organizations. It was a sign that the insurgency was shifting. As government forces repelled attacks on villages and reclaimed occupied land, the militants resorted to larger-scale violence to sow fear and chaos, to show that they would not be so easily defeated.

Once it became clear that Mohammadu's child bride was not going to bear him a baby anytime soon, the militants tried to interest Asma'u in becoming a suicide bomber. She'd seen them strap bombs to girls even younger than she was, their eyes wide with fear. They were often so skinny that they would have to wear bigger mayafis to cover the suicide vests attached to their bodies. Asma'u had no desire to follow that path. Nor did she want to become a fighter. When they tried to teach her how to use a knife to slit someone's throat, she dropped it and ran away. When they tried to show her how to fire a gun, she turned the other way. Eventually, they gave up on her. Mohammadu began talking openly about taking another wife, one who could bear children.

The days were blurring together, and Asma'u had lost interest in everything. Even escape seemed like a faraway dream. She thought about her mother and her father and her siblings. Where were they? Were they still alive? Even if she managed to leave the forest, where would she go? Was there even a home left for her?

One day, a few months into her captivity, she was getting water when she noticed a few other women looking at her. They seemed vaguely familiar, but she couldn't place them. One of them approached her as she was drawing from the well.

"Aren't you Hauwa's daughter?" the woman asked.

Asma'u froze. Hauwa. Her mother. She had not heard her name in so long. All these months of wondering where she was and here might be an answer. She stood in silence for a long time, afraid of what that answer would be. Finally, she nodded. "Yes. I'm Asma'u."

The women were from another village, they told her, but they had all been taken to the forest the same night. They said they were taken to the same camp as Hauwa after Asma'u was

BETWEEN GOOD AND EVIL

cut away from her. And then they told her something that took Asma'u by surprise: Hauwa had tried to escape. She was recaptured and taken to another camp, but there were rumours that she had managed to escape again. And another rumour that she was taken to a village controlled by Boko Haram and put in jail.

Asma'u had so many questions, but no words came out of her mouth. She had heard nothing of her family for so long that it took a while to absorb this information. The news that Hauwa had tried to escape was hard to reconcile. She knew her mother could be impulsive, but she had never imagined Hauwa would risk her life trying to escape. She thought about all the nights she'd spent waiting for the bombs to fall and the military to raid her camp so she could run. Meanwhile, her mother had decided to leave on her own. Of course she had. When Asma'u finally found her voice, the women had no more to offer. They were certain of only two things: Hauwa had tried to escape and had failed.

She asked the women if they knew anything of her sister Binta, but they shook their heads. Hauwa had only ever wondered aloud what had happened to her daughters. Asma'u asked about her younger siblings. The women said that Hauwa had tried to take them with her, but they didn't know if the militants had separated them after she was recaptured.

Asma'u shuddered at the thought of her little brother and sister being taken from their mother. She couldn't imagine that Hauwa would allow that. She decided that it would be better to believe she had taken the children and escaped again, and perhaps was now back at their house, waiting for her and Binta and their father to return.

That night, Asma'u stared wide-eyed at the top of the tarp. Mohammadu was away, so she had time to think about what she'd learned. Her mother was alive. There was hope yet that her family could be made whole. "Don Allah," she prayed. "Please let them be alive. Please let us be together again."

She was still awake when the light started to come in through the top of the tarp. Out of nowhere, there was a big explosion somewhere close. She sat up with a jolt. Another explosion, a few bangs, and the sound of gunfire.

"They're coming! Alhamdulillah! Pack up, get ready to run! The military is coming!"

This was what she had been told to listen for from the night she arrived in the forest. She looked around the tent. There was nothing she needed to gather. Nothing she wanted to remind her of this place. She stepped out into the light.

There were planes flying overhead, and the rat-a-tat-tat of gunfire was coming from all directions. The sound of explosions was far away, and the booms seemed to be coming closer. The air was filled with smoke, and Asma'u heard people coughing, children crying. But the men, the Boko Haram fighters, were mostly gone. Those who had been standing guard over the tents had already fled. Women and children were running everywhere. Asma'u took stock of the scene. She needed to run as well, but in which direction? And then she spotted Amina and Habibah, the two women who had taken her in when she first arrived.

Habibah ran toward her. "Asma'u! Come, come with us!"

Asma'u followed, and the three of them ran through the camp. There were planes and helicopters now, hovering over the area.

They were not sure which direction to go. Adrenaline and chaos kept them from seeing the path. Strangely, there were still some women in their huts. Amina shouted at them. "Come! Come with us! Do not waste this time!" The women said they would rather wait until dark. Asma'u stared at them, unable to comprehend why anyone would not take the first opportunity to leave this hell.

They ran into the forest, but they didn't know which path led the way out. Women from other camps were also in the forest. It must have been a full-scale military assault on Boko Haram's bases throughout the Sambisa. It was the exact scenario in which escape was most likely to succeed. No wonder it seemed like there were hundreds of people trying to find their way out of the forest. Once the raid was over, they could all be recaptured by any Boko Haram members who were still alive.

Asma'u thought she heard someone calling her name. She stood still for a moment and looked around.

"Asma'u!"

The voice was far away, and she couldn't place it. Was she imagining things?

"Asma'u!"

She heard it again. Different voices now, children's voices. She whipped her head in one direction and then the other, searching everywhere for the source of the voices. Once the thick smoke started to settle, she saw a pregnant woman with two children.

"Mama? Zainab? Musa?"

They ran toward each other.

"Alhamdulillah! Praise Allah!"

Hauwa threw her arms around Asma'u and started to cry.

Hauwa had spent the past several months not wanting to hope that she would ever see her older daughters or her husband again. After the militants forcibly separated her from Asma'u on that first night, she was told that Asma'u was no longer her daughter and now belonged to Abubakar Shekau. She had been inconsolable. How could this be happening? They were her children. She didn't want to believe, much less accept, that she would never see them again. The idea consumed her, so much so that she was hardly able to focus on Musa and Zainab, who were allowed to stay with her.

She was having a difficult pregnancy, as if the child sensed that his or her mother was under duress. Thankfully, the dark brown mayafi they had given her hid her growing belly. She did not want to risk the militants finding out about her pregnancy; she wasn't sure how they would treat her. Hauwa and her husband had not planned on having another child, and now she wondered if this child would ever know his or her father.

She had been held in a different part of the forest than Asma'u. But unlike her daughter, she wasn't married off to a fighter and given a tent. She, Musa, and Zainab slept in the forest under a tree. There was no shelter from the rainy season, and only leaves to shield them from the scorching days after the rains had passed. There was hardly any food, and she worried about how little she was nurturing the life growing inside her. Some days she wondered if the baby was developing at all. How cursed is a child who is dependent on a body that is a nothing but a husk of its former self? A body being starved of everything required to sustain life? Hauwa thought it might be better for the child not to be born. What kind of a life was this, under a tree in a forest?

She had tried to escape once, taking Zainab and Musa deeper into the Sambisa, but Musa had started crying, so she took them back to their tree. She thought about leaving them in the forest and running away herself. She could at least save one child—the one yet to be born. But she knew she couldn't leave them. Musa would be raised to become a Boko Haram soldier. Zainab would be married off to a fighter, and then all three daughters would be Boko Haram wives. No, Hauwa had to stay with them and hope the day would come when they could walk out of the forest together. She had already lost two daughters and her husband. She would fight to save the family she had left.

And then, after four months, her prayers were answered when she heard the unmistakable sounds of a helicopter and planes flying above the camp. But when the shooting started, Hauwa and her children had to take cover. Did the soldiers not know there were hostages in the forest? Why would they just start shooting indiscriminately? But there was no time to think. The Boko Haram fighters were shooting up at the helicopter, trying to bring it down. This was the moment Hauwa had been waiting for. She put Musa on her back and grabbed Zainab's hand. They followed the others trying to make their way out of the forest.

And then—through the fog and noise of bullets flying, helicopters circling, bodies falling, and guns firing—she saw her daughter.

At first, she thought it was a ghost of Asma'u. But even from far away, in the chaos of a military raid, a mother knows her daughter.

Their reunion seemed a miracle. To find each other in this madness. But there was no time to cry or talk, no time for questions about everything that had passed in the last four months. They were still running for their lives. The military and the militants were shooting it out, and they were in the crossfire.

"Come this way!" a man shouted at them. "There is a path here that I know. I have followed it before, and I know it leads to a road."

They followed, children on their backs, running as fast as they could. They had been brought into the forest with nothing and they were leaving with nothing but the scars on their bodies and in their souls. They were about a dozen, maybe more, as others from different camps met up on the path that promised to take them out of the hell they had been living in. At first, the gunfire seemed to fade, but then it sounded as if it was drawing nearer, so they picked up the pace. The heat was overwhelming. It was just a few months after rainy season, when the temperature climbed to the highest it would be all year. Sweat poured down their backs and their foreheads and into their eyes, but they did not stop. Exhaustion eventually slowed them down to a walk. They walked for what felt like an age, but they didn't dare stop for fear of running into more militants on their way out of the forest.

When they came to a river, several women trudged ahead on the unmarked path, choosing not to give in to exhaustion as long as there was still a threat of being recaptured. But Hauwa could not pass it by, not with two small children and one still growing inside her. She had been looking over her shoulder and was confident they had not been followed. She gathered her children around her, and they took turns washing their faces in the water, even drinking from it, to refresh and replenish. The faint buzz of helicopters could still be heard overhead, but they could no longer hear gunfire. Still, they had to be careful. They weren't out of the forest yet, and a Boko Haram camp could be closer than they knew.

Zainab and Musa were crying. They were hungry, but there was nothing to eat; they hadn't brought anything with them, and it was getting too dark to forage. Hauwa was beyond grateful to have Asma'u back. As darkness descended, they huddled against the trunk of a tree and rested, being careful only to whisper to each other, lest a Boko Haram soldier be within earshot. They knew they were taking a chance, but there was no way they could continue on in the dark. Soon, the only sound was their breath and the buzz of mosquitoes and other insects.

Hauwa closed her eyes and started to drift off. All these months spent sleeping under a tree. Perhaps she would soon be home on a mat or somewhere better than a forest floor. Suddenly, Musa started screaming and kicking, flailing his arms around his head. A bug had bitten his leg. Hauwa put her hand over his mouth to silence him. His muffled cries continued for a while, and then he was fast asleep.

They started walking again before dawn, deprived of both sleep and food. Hauwa knew they would need to find nourishment sooner than later. Musa felt like a sack of millet on her back, and Zainab had no energy to walk, even at the slower pace they were starting on. Before too long, Asma'u noticed a kadanya tree in the distance. She walked up to it and saw that the tree was full of green plum-like fruits. "Alhamdulillah," she said quietly, and then she climbed the tree to pick as many as she could hold in the folds of her mayafi.

She brought the fruit back to the rest, along with some of the tree's leaves, and then ran back to climb the tree for more. Hauwa broke open the tough outer shells and scooped out the fleshy, sweet pulp with her fingers. Zainab and Musa kept asking for more, juice dribbling down their chins. Hauwa cracked the brown nut in the middle of the fruit with her teeth and gave the kernel to the children as well. It was known to have healing qualities. They would use the leaves to wash themselves in the river. When rubbed with water, they produced a lather that was a bit like soap.

They tucked as many fruits into their clothing as they could, unsure how long it would be before they found food and shelter, and continued walking. They were now a group of about a dozen women and their children. The man who had pointed them to the path had long since disappeared. Had he gone ahead? Or stayed behind? Where were the other women who had struck out together? But there was no time to think, no time to second-guess their decisions or the path they'd taken. They had to keep moving.

They walked for two more days, following the river until it led them inland. They spent the nights quietly tucked away under the trees, waking early to continue. On the second day, they lost their way, and for a while, there was panic and confusion about whether they were in fact walking back toward the camps. Had they just walked a big circle, only to end up back where they started? But then someone spied the river, which had veered away for a few miles. They continued to follow the river—and trust their instinct that it would lead to civilization. By the end of the third day, they had finished all the fruit, and Asma'u had broken off to scout the landscape for another kadanya tree. But instead, she saw what looked like a break in the bushes. Could that be a road up ahead?

The road led to a town called Izghe, just off the Gambole River. The group's intuition to follow the river out of the Sambisa had proven right. The villagers were at first wary of the women—they were still recovering from a brutal attack by Boko Haram that had resulted in a massacre of many local people. After the women spent what seemed like hours trying to convince them, the elders in Izghe agreed to let them stay. But they were warned that they could not stay indefinitely, and that someone would contact the military to come and take them home.

They stayed in Izghe for three days. At some point, their fear of being recaptured started to subside. Izghe was a Christian town, and after they overcame their initial suspicions, the residents treated the women with great hospitality, helping them wash their mayafis and fixing them healing potions made from baobab leaves. Upon learning that Hauwa was pregnant, they gave her shelter, with her own mat to sleep on. She and the children slept as one, and for the first time in months, she felt she could breathe.

A few days later, several trucks screamed down the road and into town. At first, the women started to run, thinking it was Boko Haram, but it was the military. The soldiers had many questions. They asked where they had run from, where they wanted to go, and how long they had been in the forest. Hauwa and the other women patiently told them the story of how they were abducted and then held in the forest, and how they had escaped, thanks to the military raid several nights ago, which had created the ideal conditions for their flight. The soldiers seemed satisfied. They reached into their vehicles and gave them fresh bottles of water, warmed from the sun. Hauwa, Asma'u, Zainab, and Musa would go to Gulak in one vehicle, while the others were divided among the other trucks and returned to their respective villages. The women thanked the people of Izghe for their kindnesses, and then they all exchanged glances as they parted, an unspoken bond among the now former captives. Perhaps their long ordeal was finally over.

GAMBO

Gambo had again been given five lashes with some kind of whip, two across her back and three against her chest, for daring to leave the camp to meet a friend. She had been warned before, when she and another girl went for what they said was a walk in the forest but was actually a reconnaissance mission to scope out an escape route should the air strikes finally come. A guard had found them wandering about and dragged them back to the camp, yelling at them the entire time.

"You want the jet fighter to come? It will kill you before it kills us. And if you go out again, I will report you as trying to escape, and they will punish you."

Gambo said nothing, just gave him a defiant glare.

"You think you're so tough? If I report you and they decide to kill you, that's your issue, not mine. And don't think they won't kill you."

But Gambo was never one to take well to threats and intimidation. She and several other like-minded captives had bonded during their time in the forest, and they often found ways to meet up and go for walks. Each time they were discovered, a lashing would follow. And so it was on this day: five new scars on her body for daring to walk with a friend. She started to think that death might be better than to stay a hostage to these men. She wasn't being cavalier about it, but to yield to the rules of the forest meant giving up a part of herself, and she could not do it. It was better, she thought, to die trying to find freedom than to continue to be a slave to Boko Haram.

In time, her prayers were answered, and jet fighters appeared in the sky above her. No sooner had she looked up to say a silent *nagode* than the first bomb fell in the forest. In the subsequent bedlam, she ran away from the camp, unsure of where to go. She didn't want to make the mistake of finding herself deeper in the forest, and when she came upon another camp, she panicked a little. But then she spotted her mother. They had seen each other several times over the past few months—getting water, gathering firewood, or collecting vegetables—but they'd always had to part ways again. In the mayhem of escape, it took Hajera a few seconds to recognize her, but once she realized it was Gambo, a smile spread across her wide face. Behind Hajera were Asta and the two little ones. They threw themselves at Gambo's legs as soon as they saw her.

"Gambo, look at the ships in the sky!"

But there was no time to look up—they had to find their way out. The fighting was too intense, so they decided to shelter under a tree until the jets had flown away. When they were convinced that there would be no more bombs, they made their way through the dense bush, heading in the opposite direction from the camps they had fled.

After a few hours of walking, they came to a clearing. Gambo was now carrying one child on her back, and Asta had the other. They wandered into what looked like a camp or an abandoned hamlet. Hajera held a hand up, and silence descended on the group. She went ahead to see if there was anyone occupying the half dozen grass huts that stood invitingly after a day of walking.

It had been a Fulani settlement—six *suudu cekkes*, houses of grass mats—deserted when Boko Haram tore through the region. Hajera waved to her children; it was safe. They settled into one of the huts and prepared to spend the night, together under one roof again.

Hours later, they were shaken awake by the sound of more jets in the air and more bombs in the distance. But they knew the military would not target an abandoned Fulani colony, so they decided not to run from this place of relative safety. Not yet. They would remain here a little longer.

Later that morning, four other women and several children stepped gingerly into the clearing. "*Sannu?*" They spoke softly, fearing they had walked into a Boko Haram hideaway. Gambo and Hajera came out of the hut they had claimed. The women were wearing the same dark mayafis that marked them as prisoners of the forest. They told Hajera that they had also run when the bombs started dropping, but they had lost their way and had to spend the night in the bushes, all the while believing they were being followed by the husbands they'd left behind in the Sambisa. Hajera explained that this was an abandoned settlement. No Boko Haram members had followed them, and it was as safe a place as any to rest.

The women had millet cakes and kadanya fruit, which they'd had the presence of mind to gather on their way out of the forest. Gambo found some sticks to make a fire, over which they could warm the cakes. Asta helped the newcomers with their children. For a day, they lived together in the hamlet, sharing their stories of escape, children running around and bouncing on knees. Laughter rang out. It felt normal, or at least as normal as it could when they all knew this was a temporary stop. They relaxed, and none of them were in a hurry to continue the journey home. This moment—celebrating their long-awaited freedom—was what they had dreamed of for so many months and, for some, even years.

For one afternoon, they shared the joy of escape and the promise it held of better, more normal days ahead. They almost did not want this time to end because they didn't know what awaited them once they left this place, this state between captivity and freedom, between horror and normalcy.

They were set to start walking in the morning, but the sound of fighter jets sent them back into the huts, and they decided to stay put for another day. Not far away was a stream where they washed and took water. Finally, almost reluctantly, they left the Fulani camp, still uncertain about the direction and where this path would ultimately lead them.

Hajera remembers walking for three days through the thick brush in the forest. Gambo thinks it was longer. Hajera remembers meeting people from the Kanuri tribe. They had facial markings that distinguished them from the Hausa. She remembers staying with the Kanuri for a day or two. Gambo doesn't remember the Kanuri at all. Their memories come back together when they recall meeting some Nigerian soldiers on patrol. The men asked them where they were going and where they had come from; they told them they wanted to go to Gulak. Gambo remembers the soldiers giving them food and water, then taking them back to their village.

They both remember that the relief of being home was short-lived. They didn't yet know the trauma had already taken root inside them.

6
THE HUNTER

AISHA GOMBI surveyed the scene from the top of a large rock that seemed out of place in the expanse of flat savannah at the edge of the Sambisa forest. This was a training exercise, and for that, she was relieved. If it had been a real battle, she wouldn't have allowed the hornblower to go on for so long. She waited patiently as the man continued his chant, blowing into a goat horn. It wasn't quite the same as the traditional long *kakaki*, but the blower sounded the prayer with great flourish:

> *Oh, Allah, Oh, Prophet of Allah,*
> *Let us honour our ancestors,*
> *Oh, Allah, Oh, Prophet of Allah,*
> *Oh, Allah, Oh, Prophet of Allah,*
> *Let us honour our past kings and our current*
>   *commanders.*

Others joined in the incantation, eyes closed, feet moving. Someone lit a pile of tamarind leaves, and the men started rubbing the smoke over themselves, all the while humming their battle hymn:

> Oh, Allah, Oh, Prophet of Allah,
> Go with us into battle,
> Let us honour our kings.

Rituals were important. Aisha believed that spirits would guide them in their mission, and that the ceremony was a way of asking for help from another realm, from ancestors whose sacraments had been handed down, and perhaps from both of her mentors, wherever their spirits might be. So she waited patiently as the men finished their rites. Once she heard an opening, she motioned to the group, pre-empting a second ceremony that sometimes followed.

"Let's go."

Someone fired his gun. *Pop!* A bird flew out of a tree. Another pop. A branch fell down from that same tree. Aisha shook her head and looked at her crew. In a low, firm voice, she gave her orders: "Amina, over there. Partner with him. Jamila, he is too tall. Find someone—like him—closer to your own height. It doesn't matter if you're man or woman. In war, we are all men."

The group, about thirty in total, started to advance into the savannah, two by two, and then crouch in a defensive position, each pair shoulder to shoulder but looking in opposite directions. Everyone with their long guns ready and drawn. This is how you have to approach the Sambisa when you don't know if Boko Haram is waiting to ambush you.

Aisha kept a close eye on the group throughout the exercise, but especially on the three women. One was her cousin Amina, who'd also inherited their grandfather's tall and sturdy build. When she smiled—and it wasn't that often—her two gold teeth gleamed. She told different stories of how she had come to have those teeth. Even Aisha wasn't sure which story was true. Chinara and Jamila were younger and smaller. Chinara was twenty-three, but she looked fifteen. Jamila was twenty-five. She had wide-set eyes and lips drawn into a straight, determined line. They had not yet met the enemy, and Aisha wanted to make sure they were ready. The military had asked her to prepare her hunters for a possible rescue mission in the Sambisa the following week.

A cellphone started ringing. The familiar Nokia ring.

"Whose phone is that?" There was an edge of exasperation to Aisha's voice.

No one volunteered and the ringing was silenced immediately.

"You want to lead the enemy to us? Let's go in there—the tall grass. Protect your partner, pay attention!"

After they'd advanced several kilometres to the edge of the forest, Aisha ended the exercise.

"Good! You've done well. Let's head back and talk about strategy." She nodded toward the forest. "Next week, we're going in."

The group walked back to their vehicles parked on the edge of the main road. Aisha hung back a bit with the three women. She wanted to make sure she spoke to them out of earshot of the men.

"Before, they used to say that we women are afraid," she said. "But no more. I am so proud of you. You are going into the forest without fear."

Jamila nodded at Aisha. "May Allah protect us all, and may He grant you long life so that we can continue to work together."

"We women must work together and look out for each other," Aisha said. "But here, we are not just looking out for other women. In the forest, you must also be your brother's keeper. We are all the same family."

"We are ready for Boko Haram." Chinara still spoke with the softness of a child, but she exuded a steely determination. When the story of the female hunter first spread through Nigeria's northeast, she was inspired to follow in her footsteps to rid the country of the scourge that was Boko Haram.

Aisha's patience with her female trainees was like a gift to them. She had taught them not just how to fire a gun but how to clean it and care for it.

"Your gun," Aisha told them, "is your responsibility. It is your tool. You must treat it like a part of you. So be careful how you point it, how you carry it. We can't have any accidents."

Her lessons were more than just practical. She reminded them that they were no different from the men they hunted with, and that women were just as strong and commanding as their male counterparts. Some of the hunters were intimidated by Aisha's very presence, and she wanted to pass that confidence on to these younger women.

Aisha was, first and foremost, her father's daughter. His only daughter, and the youngest of ten children. Reflecting on it now, she could see she was raised almost like a boy. She had never held a doll until someone gave one to her own daughter. Whatever her brothers had wanted, she wanted as well. When she was barely ten, her father began teaching her to hunt. At first, it was rabbits and squirrels and iguanas, then she graduated to antelopes and gazelles. By the time she was a teenager, the long gun felt like an extension of her arm.

But over the years, the animals started to disappear—no more antelopes, no more rabbits. Too many hunters, her father said. And then Boko Haram moved into the forest. At first, the hunters and the insurgents minded their own business, sharing the vast expanse while rarely running into each other. But then, Boko Haram started to attack towns and villages.

It was a clear night in Gombi,* quiet and calm, punctuated only by a low buzzing of mosquitoes. As the hazy day faded into darkness, a cool breeze swept through the town, lulling everyone into a sweet sleep. Aisha awoke to the smell of smoke. It had to be early in the morning or very late at night. The moon was only a sliver when she got up from her bed to check on the remnants of the night's fire.

And then she heard the screaming. It came from down the road at first, and then from everywhere. Gombi was on fire. Barefoot, she ran out of her house and into the street, her heart beating faster as the reality set in.

Boko Haram had come to Gombi.

Aisha ran down to the main street, still barefoot, and saw militants in pickup trucks looting stores and setting fires. Two men were running into a shop, taking bags of millet and sacks of

* Not to be confused with the much larger city of Gombe or with Gombe State, west of Borno.

vegetables, and throwing them into the cab of a truck. A young girl was being dragged into a Toyota Hilux pickup; her father ran behind until a bullet brought him to the ground. The girl's piercing cry of fear and grief fused into a desperate wail: "Alhamdulillah! Don Allah!"

The smoke started to obscure her vision.

"Aisha!" She could hear someone yelling at her to leave the scene. Why hadn't she brought her gun?

Aisha started to pray. *Don Allah, please save us from this horror. Don Allah, please let me protect my people.* She wanted to go back and get her gun and shoot all of these militants, but she knew she couldn't. The hunters were desperate to help in the fight against Boko Haram, but at the time, the government had not yet invited them to. If she were to shoot one of these intruders now, she would be punished. So she bit her lip and watched, enraged, while her community was destroyed. She clenched her fists against the orange glow of fire and vowed she would get her revenge.

She didn't go back to sleep that night, and in the morning, she dressed and walked through the rubble to survey the damage. A quick look around told her all she needed to know. The desperate rush to bury the dead. The usual rites cast aside because there were just too many bodies. Too many bodies. No, Aisha didn't need to know more. The apocalypse had come to Gombi. She needed to act.

That very day, she approached Bukar Jimeta. Bukar had become her mentor in the hunt after her father's death.

"Bukar," she implored, "we need to take the fight to them. Look, we have hunted the fiercest creatures. Let us do this. We can take care of this. We can take care of our people."

Bukar understood. But he knew that the hunters could not take matters into their own hands. Not just yet.

"We are talking to the government," he told her. "Be patient. They will give us the permission we need. And then we will take our revenge."

But months passed, and Boko Haram came back again when Gombi was asleep. More girls were stolen, more men martyred, and Aisha had to sit on her gun. It was all she could do to not start shooting, all she could do to not grab a militant and crack his neck with her bare hands. Again, she went to Bukar Jimeta.

"Bukar, please. Let me do this."

Bukar told her he would be meeting with the government that day.

"I will make sure they deputize us now, Aisha. Be patient for just a little longer."

Aisha told him she was sure that Boko Haram was determined to take Gombi. This was a second attempt. There would be one more, and they would come prepared.

The word came down a week later. The government had officially invited hunting groups to join in the fight against Boko Haram, creating the Civilian Joint Task Force. The village elder, Alhaji Usman, told all the hunters that they should fight whenever the need arose. "Keep those weapons drawn," he said. And the hunters did. In fact, all across Borno and Adamawa States, hunters started formalizing their previously informal groups, cleaning guns that had not been used in months or years, and securing ammunition. They were finally officially in the fight. From that point on, they would be hunting men, not game. They would be defending their people, not participating in sport.

Aisha was more than ready, as she had been from the first attack on Gombi. Too many friends and neighbours had lost daughters to the forest, husbands to the cause, wives to the militants. No more. From Aisha's point of view, there was no militant group, no sect, no terrorist organization more dangerous than Boko Haram. Its fighters had tried—twice—to destroy her village. The next time they tried, they would have to come through her.

They came in the afternoon, as if to take Gombi by surprise. But they must have known the village was waiting for them because they came prepared. Aisha saw the trucks churning up the late afternoon dust. But this time, the trucks carried vats of gasoline instead of fighters. There was a pump attached to one of the vats. Aisha took a deep breath. It would be a miracle if Gombi did not burn down this time.

The fighting started right away. Someone fired into a pickup truck that did indeed carry fighters. As the wheels of that truck came to a stop, two dozen men poured out, guns drawn. And then it was chaos. Aisha positioned herself by a car, crouching down by the front tire, ready to fire at the first opportunity. All around, she heard the thud of bodies meeting the earth. The rat-a-tat-tat of rapid gunfire.

Where did they get AK-47s? she wondered for barely a heartbeat before the answer came to her. *From the government forces they killed, of course.* More screaming, more wailing. She kept firing through it all, but her long gun was not a semi-automatic like theirs, so she had to keep reloading. She cursed.

She heard an explosion, and then silence filled with smoke. Aisha knew that the gas canisters she had seen rolling into town were being put to use. Gombi's local government building was ablaze, flames licking around the front door.

The military was there as well, pushing the Boko Haram fighters into defensive positions around their vehicles. There had to be more than a hundred militants trying to take the town. Everyone seemed to be firing indiscriminately, but like Boko Haram, the government forces had semi-automatic weapons.

By morning, the surviving militants had retreated into the forest, and the locals were left to put out the fires and bury their dead. Watching it all, Aisha felt her rage growing. Why should they be allowed to get away with this? Children were burying their parents. Parents were looking for missing daughters, stolen by men and spirited to the forest, prizes in a battle they had lost. So much destruction. A communal grief descended, blanketing all that was left.

Aisha went to her commander, Bukar Jimeta, once again. "We need to stop them from coming back," she insisted. "We must take the fight to them. To the forest."

Bukar agreed. A gentle and patient man, he was enraged by the audacity of the fighters.

Aisha pressed further. "We are the hunters. Who knows the forest better than we do?"

They waited until they had information that the militants were set to return. They had left Gombi the last time without taking the supplies they needed—there was always a shortage of things in their camps. Aisha told herself there was no way she would let them come back, even if she had to go into the forest herself to stop them. Residents were still grieving, still too paralyzed to begin the process of rebuilding. Another attack would destroy them completely. The hunters were all determined to prevent any more incursions into the town. Quietly, they prepared for the fight to come, cleaning their guns, sharpening their arrows and their machetes. And when word came that it was time, they took those weapons and piled into several pickup trucks. Others perched two to three on a fleet of dilapidated motorbikes.

The fight was surprisingly easy. There was only one road leading from the forest in the direction of Gombi, and the militants were surprised to be ambushed. Jimeta shouted orders, deploying the hunters to strategically surround the enemy. The militants, despite their AK-47s and the machine guns mounted to their trucks, couldn't muster much of a defence. The hunters had braced for a fierce assault, but the fighters seemed to have been taken by surprise. They shot back, but it was too late. Boko Haram's stolen sophisticated weaponry was no match for the rough-and-ready homemade weapons the hunters had brought to the battle. They shot arrows and knocked semi-automatics out of the enemy's hands. They threatened the men with machetes. They fired homemade long guns. It was over as quickly as it had begun. The hunters gathered dozens of AKs and bound the wrists of their prisoners before loading them onto the back of their own trucks and those they had seized. They decided to leave the dead where they'd fallen. They would return to their maker in time.

After the battle, Jimeta counted his troops, his band of hunters more used to shooting antelopes than people. All were present, and none had been wounded. He wondered a little about human nature. Killing a person is very different from killing an animal, and yet his hunters had made the transition seamlessly. What this told him about human nature and conflict was a question for another day. Today, he was lucky he had not lost a single hunter. They drove their captives and the confiscated weapons to the local military station, handing everything over to the authorities.

The general in charge of the region was not surprised at the quality of weapons the hunters had seized. He had seen them disappear every time Boko Haram raided his station. He thanked Jimeta and nodded his gratitude to the hunters who were still unloading weapons. It was hard to believe that this motley bunch—a woman among them—could have stopped another attack on Gombi before it even began.

After the hunters had handed over the injured militants and all of their weapons, including the trucks they'd confiscated, they headed home. Aisha sat in the back of a pickup, her gun on her lap, empty of ammunition. The sun was setting and the sky was a deep orange. She felt a sense of satisfaction. Tonight, there would be no assault on people still struggling to recover from the previous attack. No daughters would be stolen tonight, no fathers killed, no mothers left to grieve. Today's dead lay in the forest, and they would meet whatever fate they deserved in the next life.

Aisha smiled to herself. She was pretty certain what that fate would be.

PART II: AFTERMATH

7
GULAK

HAJERA WAS RUNNING, but the bullets were getting closer. She didn't want to look behind her because she needed to focus on the path ahead. She didn't know where any of her children were; there wasn't even a baby on her back. She was in full flight and desperate to know if the children were following. She wanted to look back, but she couldn't for fear of being recaptured. This was the moment they had been waiting for. The government had come into the forest to take the terrorists away. And in that mayhem, women and children were running for their lives.

Hajera had left her eldest daughter, Gambo, in charge of her two youngest boys, Buba and Abdulmumini, while she went to fetch water. But as soon as had she lowered her water bag into the well, she heard the buzz of fighter jets and saw bullets strafe the forest. There was no time to go back to the camp, so she just started to run, hoping that Gambo and the children were also on their way.

She hadn't counted on the bombs, however, and the resistance from the Boko Haram fighters. She and the others were in the crossfire, and there was no way to find her children. She could feel the air *tightening in her chest. Where were they? This was the very scenario she had talked to Gambo about: run, no matter where everyone else is. But now, she worried her children were paralyzed by fear. She turned around—only to find herself looking down the barrel of an AK-47.*

Hajera sat up, her heart pounding, her lungs gasping for breath. How many times had she had this nightmare? All these dreams that kept bringing her back to the Sambisa. Sometimes she felt so tormented by her months in captivity that she wondered if the forest had become a part of her. Perhaps it had put down roots inside her, coming to her at night and sometimes even during the day, haunting her with memories she could not ignore. Her head was pounding, as if it might split open. It wasn't yet morning, but she was afraid that sleep would bring back more terrors, so she decided to stay awake and keep the dreams away.

She got up, poured some water from a big plastic jerry can into a bowl, and washed her face, her hands, her feet. And then she knelt for the *sallar fajr*, or morning prayer. As she did every morning, she gave thanks for her freedom, for her children, for their home. She asked Allah to watch over them and keep them all safe from harm. And then, if possible, to erase the memories of their time in the forest.

After their escape from the Sambisa, they had taken refuge in a Christian town close to Izghe. Government soldiers found them there and drove them back to their home in Gulak. When they arrived, Hajera's own mother did not recognize her.

"*Sannu, sannu*. Mama, it is me. And your grandchildren." It was only after putting a hand on her cheek and studying her face for what seemed like a lifetime that her mother embraced her and the children. Tears streamed down her cheeks.

"I feared that I would never see you again. That the forest had swallowed you forever."

To celebrate their return, Hajera's mother made soup with fish from the river and peppers picked the day before. She doted on the children, fixing concoctions from baobab and kadanya leaves, holding cups to mouths, and soothing the liquid past trembling lips and down tight throats, hoping the serum and her prayers would heal all wounds.

The children ate; it was the first real food they had been given in months. It had flavour and was tasty, unlike the watery messes that passed for soup when they were in the forest. But Hajera couldn't eat. She excused herself and went to lie down on a straw mat in another room. It felt as if someone were drumming in her brain. She shook her head several times but couldn't shake the pain out. She stared at the mud wall for a long time before closing her eyes. But she couldn't find stillness. The outline of the forest manifested itself in the darkness behind her eyes. She saw herself moving through the trees; she could smell the cooking fire she had started and hear the call of the wild birds. Her mind had travelled back to the place she'd worked so hard to leave, and she couldn't call herself home.

She's not sure how long she stayed this way. Her mother and Gambo took turns trying to reach her. "Mama, we are safe now. We are home." "Mama, look! Buba and Asta are going to go back to school." "Mama, come out. It is market day."

For Gambo, her mother's retreat into the trauma of her own mind was unsettling, to say the least. Hajera seemed vacant, unresponsive. Their grandfather had taken Buba to the village school. Asta wanted to go back as well, but Grandfather suggested she stay at home for a little while longer, at least until their mother was back on her feet.

"But how long will that take?" Asta asked.

Grandfather just shook his head. He didn't even want to imagine what they had suffered in the forest. The stories coming out of the Sambisa were horrific. He didn't want to ask the girls. He did not know how to.

And then one day, Hajera came back to herself. She got up one morning and prayed the *fajr* at dawn, then walked out of the room she had kept herself in for days. No one said a thing to her; everyone went about their day as if she had never left them. She tended to little Abdulmumini, who had been cared for by his grandmother while she was away. She watched as Buba went off to school, then turned to Asta.

"Why are you not back at school?"

Asta smiled. "Mama, I was waiting for you to come back."

It upset Gambo a little bit that no one expected her to return to school. As the eldest daughter, it was assumed she would stay home to help out around the house. But she had a right to finish school as well! Other girls her age were writing their Junior Secondary Certificate Examinations, an important assessment that would dictate their place in senior secondary school, which would in turn affect their chances of post-secondary placement. Gambo would be the first to admit she was never a great student. She liked school, but mostly for the social aspect. She had always been surrounded by friends, laughing during breaks and making faces at each other when the teacher had her back turned. She had an aversion to schoolwork, but she had never failed a class, and she could see herself studying medicine one day and becoming a doctor, highly regarded and saving lives. She wasn't sure if she would ever get there, but it never ocurred to her that she wouldn't finish school at all. So it upset her when she wasn't asked if she wanted to return. But she didn't want to trouble her mother or disturb the fragile peace that had settled over them.

Surprisingly, her Islamic education came back to her. When she was in the forest, she was in Islamic classes all day. She hated it then, but now she looked upon those lessons with a kind of wistfulness and through a different lens. She got up and filled a small plastic jug with water, then washed her face, her arms, and her feet. After laying a blanket in front of her, she knelt and said the *fajr*.

Hajera was obsessed with washing the beans. The beans had to be thoroughly scrubbed—no bits of grit, as they would add an unpleasant crunch to the cakes. Her speciality was *akara*, or *kosai*, as they called it in the north—bean cakes fried to pillowy perfection. She knew the exact proportion of beans to peppers just by looking at the mixture, and the exact consistency of the batter required to make the perfect doughnut-like ball. Before she was taken, she sold them by the roadside, fried to order, and customers told her that her *akara* was the best in the country.

But right now, she was fixated on cleaning the beans, washing handfuls of them over and over and over. "Mama, they are clean," Gambo argued. "Let's start mixing them." But Hajera kept washing. She squatted over the plastic basin and kept pouring water in, rubbing the beans with her fingers, scrubbing them between her palms, then pouring the dirty water out and fresh water in. Again and again. Each one had to be polished just so. When she was finally satisfied that she had got rid of every grain of dirt in the tub, she started removing the skins, one bean at a time, then tossing the skinned beans into another basin.

Gambo stared and started removing skins herself, rubbing a handful of beans between her palms and discarding the skins. After she had thrown the beans into the skinned tub, Hajera reached over without saying a word and removed several skins that were still hanging from the beans. Gambo said nothing but decided to continue skinning the beans her way—the way her mother used to do it. Hajera would reach over to pick out the skins Gambo had left. It was hours until she was confident that not a single skin remained among the pile of beans. She then went to get the big wooden spoon and starting mashing them.

Mashing beans should not be meticulous work. And it never used to be. But now Hajera was treating the skinning and the mashing the same way. A rough mash would no longer suffice; now each bean had to be crushed completely, and the pulp had to be homogenous, with a smooth texture. Any small lump would be beaten down, crushed against the side of the bowl.

She then chopped up some pepper and onions, again to precision, and mixed them into the bean batter. Despite—or perhaps because of—the beating they had taken, the beans were now fluffy and light, and she made sure the vegetables were evenly dispersed through the batter.

She was ready now. She laid a wet cloth over the big bowl and set it aside, then gathered the pot and oil for frying. Setting up shop just outside of their hut, Gambo lit a fire and placed the pot on top, filling it with oil and then waiting for the oil to heat. Hajera tested it by dropping a little spoonful of the batter into the pot. If it sizzled and rose to the top, the oil was hot enough.

The smell of fried cakes drew many passersby who happily handed over a few naira in exchange for a freshly fried *akara*. Murmurs of approval after the first bite. Sometimes someone would peel off a few more naira for another. Gambo took the money and wrapped the cakes in paper before completing the sale.

"*Nagode*," she would say softly to everyone, eyes downcast. "Thank you."

Business was brisk. Hajera's pot bubbled enticingly with golden orbs, shatteringly crispy on the outside and soft and creamy inside. As customers waited impatiently for their fritters to come out of the oil, it was impossible for them not to notice the vendor's daughter. Gambo was hard to ignore, despite her attempts to avoid eye contact. She was wearing a bright yellow-and-pink wrapper and had outlined her eyes with a dark pencil and painted her lips a light orange. A few tried to engage her in small talk, but she demurred, focusing intently on counting the bills and wrapping the cakes.

Later that afternoon, Gambo watched from behind the pot of bubbling oil as students her own age and younger trudged home with their schoolbooks. She saw two girls who looked familiar—did she go to school with them?—but they had already passed by. Gambo thought she saw them staring at her, but they had turned their heads by the time she registered their glances. She suddenly felt embarrassed. She should also be walking home from school with friends, complaining about homework and teachers. She looked down at her hands, greasy from wrapping the bean cakes. She should be finishing her final year of junior secondary school, not watching over a pot of hot oil and making change for a few naira. She started to say something to her mother, but then thought better of it. For the first time since they'd left the forest, Hajera had a smile on her face as she made small talk with a few customers who lingered after they had wiped the crumbs from their lips, wanting to know her secret to such a perfect *akara*. Gambo decided to keep quiet for now, but she promised herself she would talk to her mother about returning to school, like her siblings had. She didn't want to do this for the rest of her life.

When all the bean batter had been fried, Hajera packed everything up and took it all back into the hut. It was dusk, the end of a long day and the beginning of many more like it. Asta and the boys were bent over doing schoolwork. Gambo knelt for the evening prayer and then set about helping with supper, as was expected of her. She couldn't help being envious—and a little resentful—as she looked over at her younger brothers and sister. It didn't seem fair that they were allowed to go back to school while she was expected to help their mother.

Later that evening, she approached her grandfather.

"I would like to return to school to finish junior secondary, and then I have only two years of senior secondary."

Her grandfather looked at her intently. "And then what will you do?"

Gambo didn't hesitate. "I'd like to be a doctor and help people."

Her grandfather looked her in the eyes. "Maybe one day. But for now, you need to help your mother. She has suffered greatly in the forest."

Gambo opened her mouth to say "I did too!" But the words didn't come out.

And so, she continued to wash and skin beans, helping Hajera with her business. The first few weeks were busy, and the bean batter ran out early each afternoon. Gambo counted out the naira at the end of the day. The sack of beans was running low, and they had arranged for another to be delivered.

It was a different driver who brought the new sack of beans.

"*Sannu!*" Hajera greeted him, pointing him toward the back of the hut, where she would need the sack to be laid. After he set the beans down, he looked up, waiting for the cash they had agreed upon. As Hajera counted out the bills, she could feel his eyes on her, studying her closely.

"Weren't you one of the families taken into the forest when Boko Haram came?" When no one responded, he turned his attention to Gambo. "That's right. I remember seeing you in a truck with the militants. That was you, wasn't it?"

Gambo told him *nagode*—thank you—for the beans, and Hajera pressed a stack of naira into his hand. They both started ushering him to his car. But he was full of questions.

"What was it like in the Sambisa? What was it like to live with those savages?"

Hajera finally spoke. "You are mistaken. *Nagode*. Thank you."

The man took one more look at them and then got into his car and drove off.

Hajera and Gambo eyed each other nervously. They had both heard stories about the stigma that often marked those who spent time in the Sambisa. Hajera had hoped that by returning to live with her parents, and not in the house they'd fled, they would not attract unwanted attention.

Alhamdulillah, she prayed silently, *let there not be problems.*

Hajera and Gambo were now hyper-aware of every interaction, every glance—even those imperceptible to others. Their *akara* stand was still busy days after the encounter with the bean man, but over the next weeks, they both noticed that there was less small talk. Customers put their naira down and took the cakes hurriedly. Gambo kept her eyes down, feeling the heat of their gaze as if she were physically marked as having been a Boko Haram captive.

One day, they stayed out until dusk, but the bowl was still half full when they decided to finish up.

"We can add to it for tomorrow," Hajera told Gambo.

But the next day, they came home with more batter, then more and more until the day came when not a single fritter was lowered into the hot oil.

"Mama, what will we do with the batter?" Gambo could not read the stoic expression that had stretched across Hajera's face. Fanning the fire with her hand, Hajera heated the oil until it bubbled. Then she fried all the batter. There had to be more than a hundred *akara*—some misshapen, some big like discs, others just bits of over-fried dough. She laid them all out and went to her room.

The next day, after the morning *fajr*, she and Gambo looked at the sack of beans and made no movement to start cleaning them. Asta and the boys felt something was amiss, so they left early for school, taking a few fritters with them as their breakfast.

Buba came home early. They could see him walking down the road toward the house. Gambo could tell he was crying.

"Mama, he called me the son of Boko Haram and then pushed me, and I was going to push back, but he backed away from me. And then the teacher was angry with me. It wasn't my fault! He said I was a Boko Haram fighter. I was just trying to tell him that I am not, that we are not with Boko Haram. And then he pushed me again, but I didn't fall, so the teacher thinks it is my fault."

Hajera could feel her blood boiling. It was one thing for the people in the village to stop buying her *akara* but quite another for someone to accuse her son of being a Boko Haram boy. She held Buba by his arms and looked him in the eyes.

"Who said this to you? Who is this boy?"

Buba shook his head. "Just a boy in my class." He didn't know the name, or if he did, he was scared to tell his mother.

Hajera's rage only grew.

"Who is this boy?" Gambo stepped forward and took Buba's hand. "You are okay. You are not a Boko Haram son. You know that. It doesn't matter what anyone else thinks."

Buba stopped crying, but Hajera was now on a rampage. "Where are the police? I am going to report this boy. This is harassment." It wasn't until her father—Buba's grandfather—came home and put a hand on her shoulder that she stopped shaking in anger.

"Hajera, what good will it do to call the police? Buba is already guilty in their eyes."

Hajera could not accept this because it would mean acknowledging that their time in the forest—their suffering—was only the beginning of their struggle. Escaping the forest did not mean that they would escape the judgement of their community. Once you were taken to the Sambisa, you would never know peace.

"The police will have no choice," she argued. "The other boy pushed Buba."

Her father shook his head. "It is the boy's word against Buba's. And Buba was in the forest."

Hajera wanted to scream. "Maybe we should have stayed in the forest! What is this life now? How can we live like this? It is like we are marked, cursed with evil."

The following morning, Buba didn't want to go to school, but Hajera would not have it.

"You will look that boy in the eye and tell him you are my son, not the son of terrorists."

Buba shook his head. "I don't want to go today."

Gambo stepped forward and held out her hand. "I will go with you, and it will be okay. The boy won't bother you anymore."

Reluctantly, the young boy took her hand, and together they walked the short distance to the school. As they drew close, Gambo could feel eyes on them. Students, parents, even teachers turning to look at her. She started to feel a heat at the back of her neck, and an urge to tell everyone that they were the victims, not the terrorists.

Buba looked up at her, his eyes pleading with her to turn back. She heard a voice say, "Boko Haram brides are not welcome here." She looked around, ready to face the attacker, but no one took responsibility for it. Her heart started beating faster as more voices sounded their agreement. Finally, she could take it no longer. She and Buba turned around and headed home.

Hajera saw them coming down the road. She wanted to turn them back and march Buba to school herself, but something about the look on Gambo's face told her she shouldn't. Still, staying out of school was not a solution. How could they live like this, like pariahs in their own village?

When Asta came home that afternoon, it was clear that she, too, had suffered a similar experience. "We're not married to them—we never were," she protested. "And we're not going to blow ourselves up. That's crazy talk! It's not fair. We did nothing wrong."

Hajera looked at her children and then at her parents. Maybe they would have to move to another village, start over where no one knew their history. But where? And what guarantee was there that this would not follow them to the next place, like a shadow cast permanently over all of them? Asta was right—it wasn't fair. But it is impossible to argue with people who have already decided who they think you are.

Their house became known in the village as the Boko Haram house. There were a couple of other houses also marked with the same stain, and Hajera and Gambo came to know the women who lived there and had suffered a similar torture in the Sambisa. And now they were all suffering a different kind of torment, a more insidious kind that would prove much harder to get away from. Gambo started to feel a new emotion. It built up in her like the hot oil that bubbled around the *akara* batter. She swelled inside until she felt her body shake and she wanted to scream.

Rage. Red-hot rage. They had already suffered the unspeakable in the forest. To be treated like lepers in their own community was more than she could bear. If it continued, she would have to take matters into her own hands.

Gambo at her cousin's house outside Yola.

8
GOMBI

THEY HAD COME in the middle of the night and robbed her of everything she had. Hauwa still could not believe it. She wasn't sure who it was or why they did it, but they had taken all her rice, her beans, everything she used to make a living to feed her family. It was all gone. She had tried to chase them and then had reported them to the police, but there was nothing that could be done. At least they didn't find where she kept her naira. She would have to go back to the market and start anew. Yet another setback, one more among the many since she'd moved her family to this small hamlet outside of Gombi, about two hours north of Yola in Adamawa State.

They lived simply here, in a thatched hut with two small bedrooms that opened into a larger sitting area—enough for all the children and the baby boy she'd given birth to after escaping the forest. There was a space for cooking outside the hut, with stones and sticks serving as the open-fire stove. Water came from the one well in the hamlet. There was no electricity. Chickens and goats roamed freely. Like Hajera, Gambo's mother, Hauwa also supported her family by making and selling *akara*, the bean cakes that were ubiquitous in this part of the country. She was newly remarried. Her first husband, her children's father, had not been heard from since the day they were separated, and neighbours had reported that he was killed. In the forest, worrying about Binta and Asma'u, Hauwa had no time to grieve his loss.

She met her second husband when she was at the market, selling her *akara*. Abdullah had a nice smile and kind eyes, and she had noticed him watching her from a few feet away. When he sauntered over to try one of her cakes, she made sure he got one that was fried to a golden sheen and smiled widely as she handed it to him. She watched as he took a bite, waited for his nod of approval, and then said *nagode*. He was back the next day for another *akara*, and she struck up a conversation with him while she dropped the batter into the pot of oil.

She learned that he was also a victim of Boko Haram. He had been a cattleman in his village when militants looted his family home and burned it to the ground. His father was so distraught that he later died of what was assumed to be a heart attack. The militants drove the cattle away, leaving the family with nothing. Abdullah had never married. He'd spent his life helping his parents on their farm, and after Boko Haram was through, he was left with nothing. But that didn't matter to Hauwa because he made her feel heard. He didn't seem to care that she had been held captive, and that her children had been with her. He gave her the confidence to believe that her past trauma did not have to dictate her future.

Soon after they met, they got married and he moved in with her and the children. He had no money, but he gave her a great deal of emotional support. He worked around their home, helping her in whatever way she needed. She was happy enough with him, but more importantly, marrying again gave her a degree of legitimacy, a better status in her new community. With a new husband, she was not just a Boko Haram widow, not just another victim. She could almost create a new life and discard the baggage that had followed her back from the forest. Almost.

Getting to this point had not been easy. When they first came out of the forest, Hauwa, Asma'u, Zainab, and Musa were taken to Gulak by the soldiers who had picked them up in Izghe, the Christian town where they'd been staying with strangers. Life in Gulak was challenging, but they managed. In the rainy season, Hauwa headed to Maiduguri, where her ailing father lived. She worked seasonally on a local farm so she could spend half the week there, caring for him, and half of it back with her children.

After a month or so of keeping that schedule, Hauwa noticed she was being watched by some strange men whenever she arrived at her father's house. Relatives told her the men had been asking whether she was one of the women who ran from the forest. There had been whispers that Boko Haram was sending spies to try to recapture escapees. Hauwa had never believed they were that organized, but now she wondered. She decided to spend the night in the hills.

The next day, when she was at the farm picking cassava, Boko Haram paid a visit to her sick father. Hoping to put them off the scent, he told them she had gone back to Gulak. In the meantime, a neighbour ran to the fields to warn her not to return to her father's house. She heeded the warning and immediately set out for Gulak, too afraid to go back to say goodbye to her sick father.

Hauwa never returned to Maiduguri. A relative sent word the following week that her father had died a few days after she left. She found that she did not have the space within herself to mourn. There was already too much sorrow, too much grief she owed to others. When so much has been taken from you, how do you cope with another loss? She tried to take stock of everything that had been lost in the interminable months she spent in the forest, but it was overwhelming. Most of her family was gone. Five siblings. Countless nieces and nephews. If she thought about it too much, her head hurt and her breath left her.

In Gulak, rumours began to spread that Boko Haram was planning to launch another incursion. They wanted to take back some of the villages the military had withdrawn from. It was becoming a bit of a pattern. Boko Haram would overrun a village, taking the women and either killing the men or forcing them to join the cause. Then government forces would reclaim the village, chasing the remaining fighters back into the forest. But the military presence was not sustainable because there was always another town in need of liberation. The soldiers would leave, and then Boko Haram would return. And now Gulak was back in their sights.

It was exhausting. Hauwa could not think about having to run again, so she decided she would take the children and leave this place. She would never allow Boko Haram to take her back.

Hauwa and Abdullah settled their family just north of Gombi, in an informal community of mud houses with thatched roofs, off the main road leading north from Yola. Some of the women who'd escaped from the Sambisa at the same time had settled there, so Hauwa knew there would be a community—children for the younger ones to play with, and older girls who had been held in the same camp as Asma'u. It was considered safe because a local hunting group had been deputized to protect the area.

They were relatively comfortable there, but the younger children were having trouble adjusting, especially seven-year-old Musa. He had difficulty doing the simplest things. Hauwa would ask him to bring a bowl to her, and he would stare at her as if he had no idea what she wanted. He also cried a lot, flailing his arms and begging imaginary people not to shoot. She thought he must still be haunted by the executions they'd been forced to witness in the forest. Boko Haram loved to scare their captives by killing people in front of an audience. Hauwa was worried about him. The boy barely spoke, and when he did, it was in monosyllables. Asma'u had gone back and finished junior secondary school, but Hauwa could not afford to let her continue. She felt a bit guilty about keeping her at home, but someone had to help with the cooking and the chores, especially because her eldest was not there.

Thoughts of the daughter who was still missing were never far from Hauwa's mind. She could be happily chatting with customers at the market and suddenly spot a young woman she thought was Binta. As the years passed, she wondered whether she would even recognize her daughter if she returned. Binta was seventeen when Boko Haram took them all to the forest. What would she look like now, at twenty-two?

The last news she'd had of her daughter was from a woman

in Gulak who was held in the same part of the Sambisa. All the woman knew was that Binta didn't run the night the bombs fell on that part of the forest. This bit of information gnawed at Hauwa from all possible angles. Was it possible that she was still in the forest? And if so, how was she surviving? Why hadn't she tried to escape? In Hauwa's mind, there were only two answers to that question: either she was married to a commander, and thus married to the forest and unable to leave, or she was dead. But if that was the case, Hauwa believed she would feel it. If Binta had been killed, Hauwa would know; a mother would always know.

Her hope that Binta would still come home was the reason Hauwa never truly left the forest behind. Sometimes, that hope was unhealthy. She was obsessed with what might be happening to Binta and why she wouldn't have tried to escape. It was like she was missing a limb, and it was only when she went to scratch it that she remembered it wasn't there. Some days, the weight of not knowing was overwhelming. On those days, she felt she would rather know that Binta was dead so she could muster some grief and move forward. But at other times, she clung to the possibility that she was still alive and might one day walk into their home as if she had never been away. It was often the only reason Hauwa could go on. She had worked so hard to build a new life for herself and her children, but much of the time, she existed in the fog between hope and despair.

Hauwa became more devout in her prayers. She would speak to God all the time, asking for Binta's return.

Dear God, after all we have been through, please be with us, as you were with us in the forest. Thank you for bringing us out, and bless us as we continue with our lives. Take care of my lost child until you can bring her back to me when you are ready to do so. Keep her safe. Do not let her come to any harm. Please bring her back.

Asma'u could not fill that missing part of her mother's life, but she did what she could, caring for her younger siblings and helping Hauwa wash the maize and the beans in a daily ritual that she'd started to resign herself to. She longed to go back to school, but she knew it wasn't possible. She had been so happy to finish junior high school, but when it came time to enrol in the senior school, Hauwa had pulled her aside. She didn't have the money to send all the children to school, she explained, and who would help her with the *akara* business? If Asma'u spent a few months helping out, maybe their financial situation would improve and she would be able to go back to school. But for now, Hauwa needed her at home.

When the next admission period came, Hauwa was again apologetic. "Just wait for the next period, my dear daughter," she said. "By then, I will be able to afford to pay the fee and even buy you a new uniform."

And so began a pattern.

A year later, Asma'u wondered if she was destined to sell *akara* for the rest of her life. She didn't even really like the bean cakes, much less the tedious process of making them. But she had to be honest with herself—she had not been doing well in school. She had trouble focusing and found the classes very difficult. Sometimes, the teacher had to keep her after school so she could go over the lessons with her until Asma'u understood, and it often took her a long time to understand. But now that she was out of school altogether, she felt a twinge of shame whenever other girls in their small community walked by with their schoolbooks while she was out doing the washing. Going to school had given her a sense of purpose, as if a part of her old life was restored. And yet, she knew she couldn't dare to think about going back to that life right now because her mother was busy trying to build a new one for them.

Meanwhile, Hauwa's new marriage only made Asma'u miss her father more. Deep down, she harboured a faint hope that he was still alive. After all, no one had seen his body. Neighbours just assumed he was shot along with the other men when Boko Haram overran their village. But maybe he was lost in the forest, trying to make his way home? Maybe he was just in hiding, waiting for the insurgency to end?

Sometimes, while she was washing the maize or lowering the satchel down the water well or sweeping the front room, she could feel his presence. She knew that if he were here, she would be in school. He believed in the value of education. He had gone to school himself and had always told his children that they could improve their lives if they finished school. She sometimes imagined herself having a conversation with him as she went about her chores. *Papa, I want to go back to school. If you were here, things would be different. I know you would allow me to go back to school. I don't want to make akara for the rest of my life. I miss you. I miss our old life. Papa, Mama remarried, but I miss you.*

Asma'u did not resent Hauwa's new husband. In fact, she didn't feel much of anything toward him at all. Abdullah appeared one day and he was just there now, all the time. She wondered what Binta would think. Her older sister had strong opinions about everything, much more so than Asma'u, and would no doubt have had something to say about their mother's decision to get married again.

Asma'u did not mind living in this hamlet, though, where there were other girls her age who had also spent time in the forest. There was a sense of community, of people knitted together by the shared threads of loss and trauma. She felt safe here. She often saw the hunters coming through on their patrols. Somehow, their presence made her feel better, made her feel that Boko Haram could never come back for them.

Even after all this time, she was tormented by images of the forest, the dead twisted bodies she saw there. Sleep didn't come to her, and every time she made a fire, the smell of smoking wood would bring her back to the Sambisa. It was nearly impossible not to be reminded that she had lived there, smelled those things, seen those things, suffered those things. And she had a strange sense that she was being followed all the time, as if she were still running from the forest, still being chased by men who wanted to capture and enslave her again. Even when she was going to fetch water from the well, she would constantly look over her shoulder to make sure there was no one there. Perhaps, she sometimes thought, she was trying to run from the part of herself that still felt captive, the part of herself she'd left in the forest.

The older women tended to gather mid-morning, after their children were at school and their early chores completed. There was a small patch of shade in the middle of the commune, not far from the well. They sat under the grove of neem trees, barefoot, toes wiggling in the soft breeze that sometimes broke through the branches. Some days, they would sit like this for hours and not have much to say. Other days, someone might speak about the trauma that had come in her dreams the night before. Another might chime in and finish the nightmare they all seemed to share.

These women had all spent time in the Sambisa as captives of Boko Haram. Some of them had been held together in the same camp, sleeping under the same trees. There was a group of about half a dozen women—Hauwa among them—who had escaped together. But while Hauwa was taken to Gulak, the rest decided to start fresh, turning this place into a refuge for themselves and anyone else who might need a new community.

Some of the women here had been in the forest for months. Others had managed to escape after a few weeks. Most had also lost children, husbands, entire families. The collective damage that had been inflicted on them was hard to imagine. But it was something they all shared. Words were not always needed because so much was already understood. They spoke to one another from the same place.

The community kept growing. Word spread among those who'd managed to leave the Sambisa but were unable to go back to their own communities that this place was a safe haven. Newcomers arrived all the time. Josfin, a small woman who walked with a slight limp, was one of the more recent arrivals. For the first week, she sat on the edges of the gathering, watching but not speaking. Hauwa regarded her from a distance, trying to remember if she had seen her in the forest. But the harder she tried, the blurrier her memories became.

Finally, Josfin broke her silence. "I just came out from the forest last month," she said one day. Her voice was strong, but Hauwa heard a small quiver. "I couldn't go back to Kofa, my village. I tried to go there when I escaped, but Boko Haram had attacked it again. It was on fire when I approached it. I had nowhere else to go."

The women nodded in sympathy. Many of them had had the same experience.

Then her voice broke. "I left a child in there. He was just small . . ."

The women were silent, giving her space to continue.

Josfin said she was eighteen when Boko Haram invaded her life and her village. She already had a child, a boy about a year old. The militants took them both into the forest, where she was married off to a fighter. The rest of her family stayed in Kofa, living under Boko Haram's reign of terror. She didn't say much about what life in the forest was like for her, only that she bore her Boko Haram husband another son and was always looking for ways to escape. She thought she might have had a chance when the military attacked one night, raining bombs down on an area close to their camp, but her husband had stayed, not allowing her the opportunity to run. Before she knew it, five years had passed. She didn't want her sons to grow up in the forest and join Boko Haram.

An opportunity finally presented itself in the last month, when her husband took the younger boy away to meet someone. Josfin grabbed her older son and they started to walk through the camp, slowly at first, past the sleeping areas and the communal cooking area, as if they were simply going to gather wood for their evening fire. When they reached the camp entrance, there was no one there. The guards were not at their post. Josfin and her son walked out and then broke into a run once they were clear of the area. After several days of walking and resting, they were picked up by a hunter's group and brought to a police station.

"I left a child in there." She said it over and over, several times, as if she still could not believe what she had done.

The other women murmured their sympathies. Many of them also had children still in the forest.

Hauwa thought about Binta. How would she have felt if Binta had been a baby and she had to leave her? Could she have taken just one of her children, leaving the others in the forest? As it was, Binta's absence was a constant torment, and Hauwa had been able to escape, knowing she was still somewhere in the Sambisa. She couldn't imagine the depth of Josfin's anguish. Who would raise the child she left in the forest? His Boko Haram father? That would all but guarantee his fate: he would inherit his father's war and fight against his mother's children, his own brothers. It made her despair. How would this cycle of violence ever end?

Habiba, a woman who was in her early forties but looked older partly because of the crinkles around her dark eyes, shook her head and let out an audible sigh. She raised a hand and lowered it, and then, in a soft voice, she told Josfin she was not alone.

"Many of us have also left children in the forest." She gestured to Hauwa. "She has a daughter there." She nodded to another woman. "Tafisu over there, she left a son and a daughter." She pointed at herself. "Me? Two daughters still there."

Josfin met their eyes in turn.

"There is too much sorrow here." Habiba had a round, open face that held the possibility of a wide, happy smile, but her lips were taut. "Too much sorrow. We can only pray that Allah will give us some relief, that he will guide our children out of the forest. But here, we have each other. If you are thinking too much in your heart and it is giving you pain, you should just pray. And we give thanks that you are safe, that we are all safe."

The women murmured their assent and smiled at Josfin, who nodded and wiped her eyes with the back of her hand.

Josfin's son was in school with Hauwa's little boy, Musa, and later that afternoon, the two women spoke as they were getting water from the well. Two mothers in mourning for the children they'd left in the forest. Grief a lonely burden they carried separately. Hauwa felt a wave of sympathy for the younger Josfin, who looked completely lost.

"Binta. That's my daughter in the forest," Hauwa said softly. "She would be your age now. Maybe a little younger. I cannot think of what they have done to her."

Josfin looked down to the bottom of the well. Hauwa watched her carefully. It was something all the women had contemplated at some point. The well was a place where they weighed the burden of everything they had endured against what might await them in the days and months ahead.

Hauwa's voice lowered to a whisper. "We have all thought about it, Josfin. But who will look after our children? We cannot just abandon them. They need us, and we are now safe to make our lives over again. Maybe one day Binta will come out, and when she does, she will come to look for her family. We have to be here for them."

Josfin did not want to think about her Boko Haram child. Maybe it was better that she'd left him with his father. She didn't want the responsibility of having a child who might one day grow up to be a killer. How could such a hideous thing come from her? He was born an angry baby, screaming as he came out of her. But how could she blame him? Perhaps he could sense that his mother didn't want him. And yet, as horrified as she was when she'd realized she was pregnant, she eventually grew to love him. His father named him Muhammad, after Boko Haram's founder, Yusuf.

When she nursed him, she would speak to him, whispering to him, quietly pleading with him not to follow his father. She told him she loved him and would take care of him if he promised never to hurt another human being. She tried to make a deal with God, to spare the baby from the fate he seemed born into. But when the opportunity to escape came, the choice was made for her. She could not stay—not for him, not for anyone. Every day, she asked herself if she had made the right decision. Should she have waited for a time when she could take both her sons? Had she condemned her baby to a life of hatred and violence? He would grow up never knowing her, only knowing the life of his father's people. But she couldn't allow herself to think of what he might become. She kept looking down into the well, leaning into it, plumbing its depths for an answer. But all she saw was darkness.

Hauwa put a hand on her shoulder. "Come, let me make you a tea while we wait for our sons to come home."

Josfin looked into the darkness one more time, then followed Hauwa back to her house.

9
ASKIRA UBA

ZARA WAS EXCITED. She arrived early at the high school in Askira Uba, the closest one that had reopened since Boko Haram terrorized the region several years earlier. It was a co-ed school, off the main road leading into the town, with boarding facilities for both boys and girls. And it was secular. Muslim girls wore pink mayafis; Christian girls wore dresses of the same colour and material.

The hem of Zara's pink mayafi floated over the dusty path as she made her way from the school entrance to the office of the registrar, where she was greeted by a smiling secretary who put a check mark next to her name on the roster and collected the small registration fee of several hundred naira for the coming term, her second. She tried not to think about the fact that she should have been graduating, not starting senior secondary school. One of the school's vice principals assigned her a dorm, and she practically danced her way there, bag swinging from her shoulder.

Girls greeted her as she made her way to the dormitories. "Zara! *Sannu!*"

Zara laughed and returned their hellos, promising to catch up once she'd dropped off her bag.

The dorms were set a distance from the school buildings. The girls' area was made up of several worn structures with a courtyard in the middle. Inside, the rooms were threadbare. They were intended to house six girls, but they would have to sleep double that number. Zara shook out her mat and laid it out in a corner, putting her bag down next to it and saving the place for Amina, a shy girl from a neighbouring town who was her best friend at school. Her smile had caught Zara's attention on her first day back at school last fall and immediately put her at ease. As much as Zara had looked forward to going back, she was nervous. She would be older than most of her classmates, and she worried that too much time had passed since she last set foot in a classroom. But she and Amina immediately bonded after discovering that they had all their classes together. They were almost inseparable on campus, living and working and learning together, sharing almost everything. Except what Zara wanted to keep secret: her past and her real life.

It was something of a miracle that she was even here. She had always thought that she would go back to school when her daughter, Aisha, got a little older. Her parents and sister promised to look after the little girl if Zara wanted to finish her education. But there was no money for school at first; she would have to wait. And after she gave birth to Aisha, she fell into a depression. No one was left to support her educational dreams. Salamatu's husband, Dauda, who had vowed to take over from

Abdulkadiri and help pay her way, had died suddenly when he was accidentally poisoned by something he ate. Another loss for her family, and another blow to her plans for her future.

The promises made to her when she was a young girl seemed destined to remain unkept. Her father was apologetic. He would try to find the money, he assured her, but for now they just couldn't afford it. Zara had a baby and no prospects. Girls who didn't finish school always ended up married with lots of babies. But who would marry a girl who already had a baby—and worse, a baby by Boko Haram?

Then she met Bashir.

Bashir was friends with her brother Abubaker. He was a few years older, and he first noticed her when Aisha was about six months old. Zara had gone to the well to get water, and he happened to be nearby. He watched her as she carried the water home and realized that she lived in the same house as his friend. Their mother, Zainabu, was sick at the time, in bed with sweats and a cough, likely a seasonal cold. Bashir decided it was a good excuse to invite himself in, to see how Zainabu was feeling. He looked around for Zara and saw her pouring the water into jugs. She caught his stare and turned away, then picked up Aisha and disappeared into another room.

"Who's that?" Bashir asked Abubaker.

"My sister Zara."

"She's lovely. Is that her baby?"

"Bashir, she's not for you. Okay?"

But Bashir persisted. He started to follow Zara everywhere she went. She went to get water, he was there. She went to the market for vegetables, he was there, offering to carry them back for her. She refused at first, but he followed her home anyway. And then he was just there. Everywhere.

"He's following me. Is that strange?" She would say this out loud to Abubaker and silently at night to Abdulkadiri. She longed for his presence. He would have known what to do; he always had.

And then she could ignore Bashir no longer. He was always trying to make her laugh at things Aisha would do. His wide smile was hard to resist. Even Abubaker had come around to the idea of his friend dating his sister. Bashir just wore everyone down. He made decent money driving a truck from village to village, making deliveries for various businesses. One day, he drove Zara to the doctor when she had a headache that she couldn't shake. He paid for her medication and drove her home, and then just hung around until she started feeling better. He played with Aisha, who screamed in delight as he swung her up over his head and back down to the floor. Even Zara had to smile. The joy in her daughter's laughter made something sing in her own heart.

Eventually he won her over, and when he offered to help her pay for school if she wanted to go back, she was stunned with happiness.

"But I'll have to leave here to go to the school in Uba. Won't you miss me?" she teased.

"If that's what you want—to go back to school—you should go. You deserve the chance to finish high school. I'll be here on school holidays and when you get back."

"Why would you do this for me?"

"Because I love you."

Finally back in school, Zara was having trouble with her math homework, as usual. She leaned across the floor to peer at what Amina was doing and see whether she was making better progress.

Amina giggled. "Don't copy mine! I think it's all wrong."

Zara giggled, too, but copied anyway and could see that Amina had indeed got it wrong. She pointed out the mistake, and both girls dissolved into laughter.

"I should be copying from you." Amina was now busy taking eraser to paper.

Uba Secondary School was not known for its academic standards, but it was the only high school in the area. A few others had closed after Boko Haram attacked and students were taken away as captives. If the dorms were threadbare, the classrooms were worse. There was no electricity, and the rooms were in a state of general disrepair, with peeling paint, broken windows, and a shortage of desks. Students often had to share, as Zara and Amina did in English class. But Zara didn't care. She also didn't care that the dormitories were cramped. On that first day back, she was assigned to the room that Amina already shared with ten other girls. But her friend had made room next to her own sleeping mat for Zara, who had arrived with two big bags full of clothes, snacks, and other necessities that her parents and sister had sent with her. She had a new used cellphone, which she used to call home if she felt lonely or missed Aisha, who had just turned three and was now living with her parents.

It sometimes felt to Zara that she was leading a double life. She was a student like the other girls, dressed in a pink headscarf and mayafi, going to classes, doing homework, and living the life of a carefree teenage girl. But what no one at school knew was that she also had a daughter at home, and she had once been held in the forest by Boko Haram. She didn't want to tell anyone, for fear of the stigma that marked so many other survivors of the forest. She didn't want anyone to know she had a child born of the forest.

In the beginning, she had always told herself that Aisha would know the truth one day, but as her daughter got older, Zara began to change her mind. She didn't think it would be fair to force Aisha to bear the burden of knowing she was the daughter of a Boko Haram fighter, a man she would never meet.

So she kept this past trauma a secret—even from Amina— and focused on being a student again and calling her family once every few days to hear Aisha's voice.

She usually made those calls at night, long after classes had ended for the day and following the evening meal. Each night, the school gates were firmly shut to deter kidnapping attempts. The school had adopted this practice back in 2014, after the Chibok incident, but they had never gone back to leaving the gates open, even now, years later. Boko Haram was still active in the region, and the school was not going to take any chances. The threat was indeed ever-present, and it sometimes kept Zara awake at night, when the forest would come back to her. The soft snoring of her dormmates did little to distract her from her memories. Some nights, she lay awake staring at the ceiling, the same way she used to stare at the ceiling of the hut in the forest. And projected on the ceiling in the dormitory, she could see the images in her mind: the hut, the guards, the guns. Running through the thick bush. She could see herself being beaten by a guard, by the husband she was forced to marry. She closed her eyes, but the images did not disappear. They just played on a continuous loop until her mind was exhausted and she drifted off into a restless sleep.

During the day, not a single one of her roommates was any the wiser, and Zara was able to forget the memories that haunted her nights as she went from lesson to lesson, laughing and bantering with friends. But it was hard, this double life. She would often call home when she had these thoughts, hoping that the sound of her daughter's voice would magically make the nightmares disappear. She needed someone to talk to, someone to validate her fears, her nightmares. A doctor of the mind, she thought, would help her control her runaway thoughts. But she knew that wasn't possible. They only had such doctors in the south, in places like Abuja and Lagos, where people had money to pay for such luxuries. Here, they could barely afford to see a doctor for the pains that ailed them physically. Zara resigned herself to living with the dreams, lingering reminders of the horrors she witnessed in the forest. Her mind would not let her forget, and perhaps that wasn't a bad thing. Someone had to remember those who would never come back.

When Zara came home for school holidays, Aisha shrieked with joy, running into her arms. It was as if no time had passed between them at all. But Aisha had grown in Zara's absence. She was definitely a little taller and was speaking in short sentences now.

Some things had not changed, however—including the way the community treated her. She still felt reproachful eyes following her when she crossed the street or went to the market.

She remembered how she had stayed at home after giving birth to Aisha, out of fear of further condemnation by the villagers. She also had an irrational anxiety that the baby would somehow understand that she had been conceived in violence. Those attitudes in the village remained, and this made Zara angry. Eventually, the village chief had to intervene and explain that what had happened to Zara was not her fault. He told everyone to stop abusing her in public. But no one listened.

Stories of girls who had been taken by Boko Haram and then deployed as suicide bombers were travelling across the region. There was one story about a girl who was sent into a market to blow it up, but when she got there, she saw her own family. When they went to embrace her, she panicked and detonated herself, killing her family and everyone around them. Who knew if it was true, but these anecdotes were all the evidence that people needed to condemn any girl who had ever spent time in the forest. When they looked at Zara, her neighbours saw not an innocent and hard-working schoolgirl but a terrorist-in-waiting, so they kept their distance and continued their whisper campaign about the "Boko Haram wife" now living in their town.

It bothered Zara more now than it had when she first came back from the forest. She had done nothing to make people believe she had actually volunteered to join Boko Haram, and everything to try to make them see that she was moving forward—going to school, being a good mother when she was home. But none of that seemed to make a difference. Old friends from school crossed the street when they saw her approaching. Sellers at the market would cover their wares when she passed. Everyone had made up their minds.

Everyone except Bashir.

He kept coming around, and Zara learned from her parents that he had been coming by the entire time she was in school, bringing treats for Aisha and sometimes fresh fruit from his parents' garden.

"He's a good man," Zara's mother would often whisper. She would nod in agreement, but deep in her heart, she knew she wasn't ready to marry. She wanted to finish school first.

Also, Bashir, for all his affection, had not mentioned marriage. On this visit home, she found out why.

"I'm joining the military." His voice was barely a whisper.

It took Zara a minute to register what he'd just told her.

"No! Why?" Her thoughts started racing, and her heart skipped a beat.

"I know, I know. But it's what I want to do. It's how I can help the country fight back against this scourge."

"You know what happened to Abdulkadiri! I lost him after he joined." Zara stared straight at him, willing him to deny her the loss she still felt.

Bashir couldn't argue with emotion and past trauma, so he stayed silent and took comfort in the fact that her concern meant she cared far more about him than she would ever let on.

As the day approached when she would have to go back to school, Zara grew melancholy. She played with Aisha and pleated her hair into thin braids, holding her close and bending over to breathe in the scent of her. She told herself that by completing her own education, she was doing something for her daughter. She could send Aisha to school as soon as she was old enough. She had to do this to secure their future.

She squeezed Aisha tight and tickled her toes. The little girl squealed with laughter. Zara tucked the tinkly sound of her glee into a corner of her mind as well. It would help her through the next few months, until they could be reunited.

Zara with her friend Amina at Uba Secondary School in Askira Uba.

10
MISSION: SURRENDER

MAMA BOKO HARAM was rushing to meet someone she had been trying to enlist to help her negotiate the surrender of a senior Boko Haram commander and the release of the remaining Chibok girls. It was May 2019, more than five years after their kidnappings. And she was losing patience with this person. This was her second time asking, but it was still the best opportunity she could see to break the stalemate that had settled over this case. She had to keep trying.

"Hurry," she told the driver, fanning herself in the passenger seat. An intense heat wave was suffocating all of northeastern Nigeria, even though summer was still weeks away. The temperature was oppressive and seemed to slow everything and everyone down. It didn't help that Maiduguri's roads were, as a rule, governed by chaos: people darting into traffic to cross streets; goats wandering aimlessly everywhere. Each driver seemed to make his or her own laws.

After what felt like an eternity, she arrived at the entrance of what looked like a refugee camp, except that it was for Nigerians who had been forced from their homes and communities—the internally displaced—mostly because of Boko Haram. Many informal camps had been set up across the northern part of the country for these people. This one was a sprawling, makeshift mass of tents and mud walls in northern Maiduguri.

She got out and was immediately greeted by the camp elder, who had been expecting her. As they spoke at the entrance, children gathered, curious about this visitor whose face was completely hidden under a black veil. A small boy ran toward her. He was wearing only a pair of brown shorts, his swollen belly protruding over them, the telltale sign of malnutrition. Two slightly older girls, clothed in matching bright orange and green wrappers, followed, chasing after him. Their eyes were wide and searching as they stared at Mama.

It wasn't her first visit to this camp. Complete Care and Aid, the foundation she'd started for victims and former members of Boko Haram, had been helping support this place, but it wasn't a regular stop on her schedule. Mama interrupted her chat with the camp elder to bend down and greet the children. It always pained her to see children in these places. She wished there was more she could do for them, but the scope of the displacement, the insecurity, and the sheer need was overwhelming.

A young woman wearing a blue-and-white patterned headscarf had come to the entrance to meet Mama. She stood silently while the older woman was speaking to the children. Her jaw was set tight and her eyes darted nervously, as if she was unsure where to set her gaze. Mama took her time with the children, then the camp director ushered them all down a narrow alley between makeshift tents and mud walls. Chickens scampered underfoot, squawking as they were chased through the dusty passages by giggling children. Skinny goats bleated as they too were pursued. The smell of maize cooking, the gurgle of water boiling over a wood fire: the smells and sounds were always the same, but this place could feel different every time. The camp was a labyrinth of thatched walls, corrugated tin roofs, and clotheslines hung with colourful wrappers, shorts, and shirts. There were thousands of people living in this inhospitable place; each one was an individual, distinct from the others.

"Mama! Mama!" A person was yelling from somewhere in the distance. Word of Mama's presence in the camp had spread, and everyone wanted an audience. People seemed to believe she could personally lift them out of this place and into a safe new home. It was hard for Mama to ignore the calls and press ahead, but time was short and she was here for a reason.

The elder stopped at the doorway of a mud structure, and Mama stepped into what was akin to a front room. The corrugated tin roof had been raised so that air could circulate through the space between it and three mud walls. The fourth wall was set back, with openings leading to two dark rooms.

The young woman in the blue-and-white covering had been following the group as they made their way through the maze of living quarters to this space. Her space. Her home.

She stepped forward now and spoke one of the few words she knew in Hausa.

"*Sannu*, Mama."

Because she had grown up in the south, Mama's mother tongue was Igbo. Hausa, one of the dominant West African

languages, was most widely used in northern Nigeria. Boko
Haram's leader, Abubakar Shekau, was from the Kanuri tribe
and spoke that dialect, along with Hausa. Many of his acolytes
also spoke Kanuri, which is another language commonly used
in northern Nigeria and also in parts of Niger, Cameroon, and
Chad, around the Lake Chad area. Despite having married into
a Kanuri family many years ago, Mama still found it such a hard
language to grasp, but she had come with Hassan, an older gen-
tleman, an elder himself, who was working with her foundation
on a rehabilitation program for former Boko Haram soldiers.
He spoke Kanuri, Hausa, Igbo, and English perfectly and would
serve as her translator for this visit.

"*Sannu*, Nneka," Mama said. "When was the last time you
spoke to your brother?" She waited while Hassan asked the
question in Kanuri.

"Last month."

"Did you tell him what I said?"

"Eh. I told him. I told him that Mama wants peace, and that
you will take care of him like you took care of us, and that it is
better to live here at home than it is to stay in the forest."

Mama smiled at this. But then she remembered that she had
asked for something specific.

"I asked him to send a video of himself with the remaining
Chibok girls, and to release three of the girls to me, to prove
himself. Why didn't he send the video? Or let the girls come?
The video will prove to me that he is willing to deal, to talk.
Why didn't he send it? Why does he not trust me?"

Hassan translated the questions in a calmer voice than Mama
had used.

The younger woman looked a little confused. She wasn't sure whether she had forgotten about the request or her brother had forgotten to make the recording. She hedged in her answer.

"Eh. It's because the video of the girls had already been done. They did discuss it, but they decided they did not want to send it and wanted me to go get it and bring it to you instead. And I would have to come to get the girls."

Mama frowned. The girl's brother was a very senior commander in the forest, second only to Shekau, and had been a central figure in the Chibok kidnappings. If she could negotiate his surrender and the rescue of the remaining girls, it would go a long way to cementing her reputation with the government. More secure funding might follow. And more militants might be rehabilitated. This video was an important step in that process.

"Do you know for sure that the Chibok girls are with him? He can show me he can be trusted by allowing the three girls to come. He doesn't have to come with them, but he can just send three to start with."

Nneka nodded. "Yes. I have seen them. And I think he will release the three girls to you."

"Do you know where he is?" Mama pressed.

"Eh." Nneka shrugged.

"Still in the forest? Have you spoken with him lately?" Mama looked at her closely.

"Eh." Nneka looked past Mama's shoulder.

Mama wasn't sure she could trust her. The girl had been married to another senior commander in the organization—reportedly also involved in the Chibok kidnappings and behind some of the major bombing attacks in Abuja—before he was killed in a government air strike. It was only then, after her husband died and she was left with few options, that she had asked for help to leave the forest with her two children. That was four years ago. Mama had managed to find them a place at this camp. She thought she would have made better progress by now in recruiting her to bring out more captives and commanders. But Nneka was difficult to read and nearly impossible to understand, and her circumstances had not improved since she'd arrived here.

The conditions at this IDP (internally displaced persons) camp, while not the best, were at least slightly better than those at most of the informal camps that had sprung up all across northeastern Nigeria. Still, Mama worried that the girl would lose patience here and decide to take her children back into the forest. That was happening more often with girls who had escaped or been rescued from Boko Haram. They were becoming increasingly frustrated with life outside captivity: the ostracism of the community, the lack of resources, the inability to return to their homes. Women like Nneka, who'd had a position of relative stature inside the forest, were often more comfortable there.

Mama was about to hand the girl a few thousand naira when two messy children ran into the room.

"*Sannu* to Mama, please." The younger woman gestured toward their guest.

"*Sannu*, Mama!"

Mama hugged the two children, making a special fuss over the older one and asking her about school. Unlike the informal camps, this one had a school for children living here. *It isn't so bad*, Mama thought, as a chicken wandered into the space.

Other people were starting to gather around, and Mama knew that soon she would be surrounded by others looking for help.

The children ran off after the chicken, which was exiting through the entrance in a hurry.

Mama pressed the bills into the young woman's hand and looked at her. "Is there anything else you need?"

Nneka shook her head. She looked at Mama with a gratitude she could not express in words. She wouldn't be here without Mama's help, and having lived several lifetimes and witnessed so much horror in her twenty-five short years, she didn't trust anyone else. She didn't speak much about her past, and when she did, she often lied, telling people that she had married young, at the age of fourteen, and that her husband had joined Boko Haram shortly after that. But Mama knew the truth: she had been kidnapped at sixteen and taken to the forest, then married off to a fighter who rose to become Abubakar Shekau's most trusted commander. Soon, her brother joined them as well, working his way up to be another of Shekau's senior commanders.

Nneka was there—peripherally—at almost every meeting, overhearing their conversations about strategy, about which towns were easy prey and where they could find the generators, cars, and weapons they needed in the forest. Her life was markedly different than the lives of most girls in the Sambisa. She was married to a commander, and girls would be brought to help her look after her children, cook dinner, clean her home. Her husband would come back from night raids on nearby villages with lavish gifts of jewellery, watches, cellphones, and other things they stole. They lived not in a hut but in an abandoned building that had been turned into a home.

She lived comfortably enough, but deep down, she also knew it was not right. Yet for four years, she said nothing—not even when her husband returned to the forest one night with almost three hundred hostages from a school in Chibok. She had looked at the frightened girls, some of them crying, and turned away. But she could not turn away from the screams of girls being violated, from the sadistic laughter of the violators, from the painful whimpers after they left. It made her feel sick. She could no longer ignore the bodies that had piled up in the pit, the executions that took place frequently and violently, the blood that stained the ground on which she walked. What kind of life was this? It sometimes seemed to her she was living with savages. Worse, her brother and her husband were among the perpetrators—no, the architects—of this evil.

Looking back now, Nneka couldn't believe she'd lasted so long in the forest. How had she managed, especially with two babies? She did know that she'd promised herself she would not allow her children to grow up belonging to Boko Haram. When her husband was killed, she knew she had to leave. That's when she reached out to Mama. And now, the older woman needed her help.

"He's tired of fighting, isn't he?" Mama's voice was a whisper through her face covering.

Nneka nodded.

Mama shook her head. "They all are. How long can they go on like this? I have heard that they are running out of food."

"Eh. They were always running out of food."

"But he is tired of fighting. Will he come out of the forest?"

"He will come if you help him, Mama."

"Tell him to come. He will be safe."

The older woman bit her lip after she made that promise. She knew in her heart that she couldn't guarantee the safety of any Boko Haram fighter who wanted to surrender. Not so long ago, she had worked to negotiate the release of a dozen fighters, with an understanding from the government that they would be taken into custody and tried. Instead, when they came out of the Sambisa, guns laid down, the Nigerian military summarily executed them and then put out a press release saying they had killed a dozen Boko Haram members.

Mama could not believe what had happened. She felt betrayed, and she was afraid her "sons" would see her as the betrayer. She was on the phone immediately, calling people in the government, demanding an explanation. No one responded. She suspected that the authorities had done this on purpose to undermine her influence with the group, which was misguided. She didn't understand why they wouldn't work with her. Months of work to negotiate this surrender—trust that she'd built between the government and the fighters—extinguished in an instant.

She was so angry that she wanted to stop trying to help. But she couldn't. After all, they were her sons, her boys. There were just too many fighters who needed her help to quit Boko Haram, and now she was able to offer them a safe place to go. The Complete Care and Aid Foundation was established on the premise that no one was beyond salvation, and that rehabilitation was possible for those who were willing to renounce their affiliation with the terrorists. The foundation was really her last hope at brokering reconciliation.

It was easier for Mama when Muhammad Yusuf was the leader of Boko Haram. She had channels to him. Even if he ignored her—even if she felt he was lost to her—she somehow still felt a connection. After all, he had eaten her meals, had stood at her door, and had come to see her when she asked for him.

But Mama knew it couldn't last. By 2009, relations between the government and Boko Haram had deteriorated to the point that they were on the precipice of an all-out war. Operation Flush was promoted as an effort to target criminals who were bullying residents across the country, but in practice, government forces kept their focus on the northeast while ignoring similar crimes in the south. Yusuf believed the operation was really an excuse to go after him and his followers. And he was determined to fight back.

That June, some of Yusuf's followers were riding their motorbikes in a funeral procession to bury friends who had been killed in a road accident a few days earlier. The police stopped them because they were not wearing helmets. A scuffle broke out. Shots were fired, and more than a dozen Boko Haram members ended up in hospital. Yusuf was out of town, but it didn't take long for word to reach him. As far as he was concerned, the government was goading him, trying to provoke a confrontation. Yusuf was more than happy to give them what they wanted.

Mama wasn't there when he delivered his infamous "Open Letter to the Nigerian Government" speech. She heard about it later. It was all anyone was talking about. In hindsight, she could see it for what it was: a declaration of war.

"Yesterday . . . some of our Muslim brothers were on their way to perform burial rites for four corpses of our brothers [after departing] from the Ibn Taymiyya Center in Maiduguri," Yusuf declared, "when they ran into a detachment of Nigerian soldiers and the Mobile Police . . . They opened fire upon our brothers with their guns, shot them with their bullets."[6] The crowd booed. Yusuf continued, "This is exactly how they will come to our [Ibn Taymiyya] study center and shoot, if we allow them. This is also exactly how they will abuse our women and terrorize them if we leave them. I hope it is understood . . . We will rather sacrifice our lives. It is better we do not live in the world at all."[7]

Later in the speech, he addressed the authorities directly. "You should prepare your guns," he warned, "because we know you are preparing. Some days back, during their training, one of them said that they would get rid of us very soon. We know for sure that even if you attack us with all your military strength and planes, those who will survive will continue, and not hesitate to wage jihad."[8]

Mama watched all this with a sinking feeling in her heart, and her worries only grew when some of her boys turned up at her compound one day in a military vehicle.

"Look, Mama! We took this from the government forces!"

She was incredulous. "What do you mean you took it?"

But the boys were joyous. They had killed the soldiers in the vehicle and then took it for a joyride, ending up at Mama's in time for lunch.

"You can't keep this!" Her voice was firm, but she was feeling faint. "What do you need a vehicle like this for?"

"For jihad, Mama!"

And then they went for their afternoon prayer. Curious, Mama followed them.

"Allah, forgive us! Allah, give us strength! Allah, peace on their souls!" The boys were hitting themselves and crying up to the sky. "Allah, forgive us! Allah, save our souls! Allah, peace on their souls!"

Mama couldn't understand it. They were asking forgiveness for killing the soldiers and praying for the souls of those they'd slaughtered? She wanted to ask them why they would kill if they knew it was wrong, especially if they were asking for forgiveness after. Instead, she watched them as they prayed, no longer able to recognize them. She studied them as they ate her goat stew, just as they had for years, but she didn't know them anymore. They had gone from her. Something was inside them, something she could not grasp. An evil had entered and was growing.

The following day, they attacked a police station in Maiduguri, killing several officers. The battle Yusuf had promised had come. For several days, the city was under siege, almost locked down, as Yusuf and his gang set upon neighbourhoods and houses, killing and burning indiscriminately. Dead bodies littered the streets, lying in pools of blood that had gushed from their open throats.

Mama despaired. That kernel of cold fear she'd felt when they drove up in that military vehicle was now a full-blown panic. Everything she had dreaded was coming to pass, and more quickly than expected. She tried to reach Yusuf one more time, but he was too focused on taking the fight to the government. When he ignored her, she prayed. She couldn't understand what kind of God would allow His believers to kill in His name. She recalled a conversation she'd had with Baba Fugu, Yusuf's father-in-law and her spiritual leader. She wanted to know how someone could slaughter and kill in the name of Allah. Where in the Qur'an, she asked him, does it give anyone permission to take another life?

Baba told her it was simple. "They are brainwashed into this belief. They are using the Qur'an to justify their actions."

It was a concept Mama couldn't grasp at first, but as a former Christian, she knew that all religions have since the beginning of time been used to justify the most heinous acts. It made her wonder whether she could use that same religion to bring them back. If Islam could tear her boys away from her, turn them into killers she no longer recognized, it could certainly bring them back to her. It wouldn't be easy, but she had to try.

Meanwhile, Yusuf was determined to finish what he'd started. He had to wage his jihad. As Maiduguri burned and bodies piled up, Mama sensed it would end quickly for him. And it did. It came when they finally raided his compound, looking for him, burning everything down, as if fire would cleanse the city of this scourge. But Yusuf was not there. He was at his wife Amina's house, in hiding, and when police eventually found him there, they dragged him away. Mama is still not sure what happened after that. No one knows, except the police. The next thing she heard, Yusuf was dead. Worse, they had also killed his father-in-law, Mama's beloved Baba. Her grief was overshadowed by her fury at the stupidity of the government forces. Yusuf was now a martyr, and his followers would become even more disaffected, violent, and bent on revenge.

The government might have thought that killing Yusuf and destroying his mosque would be the end of Boko Haram, but when Abubakar Shekau emerged as Yusuf's successor the following year, Mama wasn't surprised. After all, nothing had changed for the surviving members of the group. They were still uneducated, unemployed, young, angry, and armed. And now they were also determined to honour their founder's memory. Her boys were now fully under the influence of someone she didn't know and had never met, and she didn't know if she could ever bring them back.

As Shekau began to solidify his leadership, Mama started to notice a gradual shift away from Yusuf's preaching and toward a more tactical, terrorist approach to establishing the Islamist state Boko Haram wanted. Surprise attacks, like a prison break in the city of Bauchi to free hundreds of suspected members, caught authorities off guard. Assassinations of aid workers, mass killings of students, and bombings of churches became trademarks.[9] And then, in the summer of 2011, they struck the capital, Abuja, with two suicide bombings—of the United Nations country headquarters and the national police headquarters. Shekau's profile was as menacing as it was prominent. He and Boko Haram were beginning to garner the attention of the international media.

Mama was pained. She reached out to her boys—those she still had influence with—to plead with them to leave the group and come home. She would provide for them, she promised. She would house them, give them money, send them to school—whatever they wanted, if they would only leave. She even started selling some of her own belongings so she would have cash on hand. She thought that if she could convince a few of them to lay down their weapons, more would follow. But during those early Shekau years, very few did. Caught up in the rapture of their jihad, they mostly placated Mama by telling her—unconvincingly—that they were doing good works in the forest. "Mama," they would say, "we are doing this for the good of everyone." There was little she could say to make them see otherwise. They were all brainwashed, she kept thinking. Baba Fugu had not been wrong. In a way, she was relieved he wasn't alive to witness what was going on.

She didn't know it then, but her sons were now members of the most feared terrorist group in the world. In April 2014, they would be catapulted into global notoriety with one spectacular act: the attack on the girls' school in the town of Chibok. Mama was stunned. It seemed the boys were getting bolder, encouraged by Shekau's fiery rhetoric. And now nearly three hundred families were missing their daughters.

Mama felt sick. She started calling her sons right away. At this point, she wasn't even thinking of negotiating with them to release the girls. It was more of a desperate plea for them to do the right thing. But her entreaties went unheeded, and the violence continued. Every week, it seemed like another village was burned, more girls were taken into the forest, more government forces were killed. When would it stop? she wondered. How would it end?

Her sense of dread manifested in health problems, including high blood pressure and heart palpitations. Doctors prescribed pills and rest. But her mind could not rest until there was peace. It was as if her body was physically shuddering under the weight of what was happening to her sons, to her country.

"Mama, I will go and give him the message."

Mama turned her attention back to the young woman at the camp. Nneka said she would leave the next day for the forest to try to talk her brother into surrendering.

"He will only come to you, Mama."

"Tell him he can come stay with me if he wants." If he came out, she would work on deradicalizing him herself. She would use the Qur'an to rehabilitate him; she liked to think of it as reverse brainwashing.

"Yes, Mama."

She looked at the girl closely. Her dark eyes seemed sunken, both wary and weary—dark pools holding secrets, as if trying to forget the things they had witnessed. Mama had known Nneka since she came out of the forest four years ago, after her husband was killed by government forces. He was by all accounts a monster who likely did not treat her or the children she bore him very well. Or at least that was the story she told. Who knew what the truth was? It sometimes seemed to Mama that Nneka had brought a part of the forest back with her, a part that the older woman could not reach, no matter how hard she tried.

But now, as Mama sent her on a mission, back into the Sambisa, she looked into those dark pools. This time, instead of looking away, Nneka returned her stare, as if to say, "Yes, I will do my best, Mama."

"Call me when you get to him."

11
THE HUNT

THE QUEEN HUNTER was ready. More than simply prepared to fight, she was eager to apprehend any Boko Haram fighter who was ready to surrender his weapons and repent for his actions. She would frequently talk to village elders to learn what they were hearing from the forest. They were her spies on the ground, her eyes peering into the darkness. She took her position very seriously, as did the elders, who trusted and respected her. After all, it seemed that Aisha's rise from antelope hunter to one of Boko Haram's most feared adversaries was almost predestined.

Apart from her father, there was only one person in the world whom she admired without question, who inspired her to put justice ahead of fear and bravery ahead of her own selfish needs. Although he was an old man now, Mai Ajirambe had been one of the first leaders of the hunter group that Aisha eventually joined. By the time the government had invited local hunting groups to join in the fight against Boko Haram, Mai's name and reputation were legendary. He grew into old age with the kindness of a grandfather and a knowledge of the land that rested deep in the marrow of his weary bones. He wasn't going into the forest anymore—his aging hips and slow gait would have been a burden on his troops—but he would accompany them to the edge and give them words of encouragement before letting them go on without him. He had shrunk a little with age, but he still cut a commanding and compassionate figure. He was a natural mentor to those who followed and trusted him. The hunters and the huntresses. He believed there was a sacredness in what they were doing, whether it was tracking big game in the wild or terrorists in the forest. He loved the ritual: the strategy meetings in the days before, the smoke ceremony at the edge of battle, the unity of purpose in the mission. He had instilled in his acolytes the value of kinship and the respect required for the animals at the other ends of their weapons. Yet this was a different kind of hunt. They were vigilantes now, defenders of their families, of their villages, of their poor but peaceful existence, and they were facing killers who lived by different values. More than anything, Mai wanted to join the battle, but he understood the limitations of his own body. For that, the old *oluko*, the tutor, put his trust in a younger man who had become the obvious choice to take command.

Bukar Jimeta's face was thin, with cheeks that appeared slightly concave. He dressed like a soldier, in green fatigues and with a bandolier of shotgun shells strapped across his chest.

The Nigerian military had been given American drones to use in their search for the Chibok girls a month after their kidnapping in 2014 and had spotted what appeared to be several of them wandering around the forest. They must have escaped and were lost, trying to find their way out. From the air, the terrain looked endlessly the same, but the hunters had pinpointed their location and were sent in on a rescue mission. The old man left his troops after the smoke ceremony, watching as they disappeared one after the other into the Sambisa. He felt a sense of responsibility—perhaps even guilt—at leaving them, but his anointed successor, Bukar, was a capable leader, and he was in charge now. Mai got back into his truck, reluctantly.

Bukar knew the forest as well as his mentor did. He knew exactly where to go. The maps the military had shared with him were clear in his head. The hunters paired off and began a slow and cautious advance into the woods, ever aware of being surprised by a Boko Haram ambush, using the girls as bait. It had become obvious in recent months that the hunters were being targeted themselves. Boko Haram, enraged that the government had enlisted the help of these vigilante groups to dislodge them from the forest, considered them enemies, agents of the state they were at war with.

After leaving the hunters in the forest, Mai drove along the main road to Maiduguri. His small hamlet was only about ten kilometres from the state capital, and the plan was to meet his team later at the police station when they handed the rescued girls over to authorities. He didn't notice the car that had turned onto the road and was now following him.

Aisha remembers when she first saw the girls and gently encouraged them to come out of hiding. They were small figures, tentative and afraid. She told them they would be safe. They looked so skinny, so scared, shrunken as much by fear as the torture they had endured. When she asked them their names, they spoke so softly that she had to get them to repeat themselves several times.

The hunters put the girls in their vehicles and drove out of the forest. When they handed them over to the authorities at the police station in Maiduguri, a few local journalists asked them about the rescue. Where had they been found? Was it difficult? Were there more girls in the same area? But the hunters were preoccupied with something else: Mai Ajirambe had not met them at the station. In fact, he was nowhere to be found.

They recovered his body the next day. He was left out in the open, off the main road to Maiduguri, just off a small road leading to another village. He was lying torso down. His decapitated head had been placed deliberately on his back. Boko Haram's message was menacingly clear: We are coming for you. Nobody is safe, not even an old man.

Bukar was too angry to mourn his mentor's death; he was filled with a vengeance that overpowered his grief. As an esteemed elder in their small community, Mai deserved a natural, dignified death. This cruelty was barbaric, a godless, cowardly act by men who called themselves good Muslims.

In a dark corner of his mind, Bukar could see the old man being surprised at his own house and taken away at gunpoint. He shook his head, trying to keep the next frame from coming into his mind's eye. He didn't want to think about the horrible torture, the mockery and humiliation Mai must have suffered at the hands of his killers. He preferred to imagine the old man keeping a stoic and dignified silence as his blood drained away, ready for the next phase of his journey, where his soul would find peace.

In Bukar's own journey, the next phase was driven by raw, hateful rage. Boko Haram had to be stopped. That was his mission, and he would do it with or without the other hunters by his side. Perhaps it made him careless or fearless, obsessed by a primal need for revenge. Too quick to leap when he should have crawled on his belly. The hunters understood they were now targets in this brutal war for control of their farms and villages, their wives and daughters, their sisters and brothers. Lose the land, lose their families, and there was no reason to live. They had aligned themselves with the government forces, sharing intelligence and leading the police to Boko Haram camps. To their enemies hiding out in the Sambisa, they were collaborators, and all collaborators must die.

Slowly, and without much notice, the hunters started moving their families out of their villages and into bigger cities, where it was safer. Maiduguri. Yola. A precaution against almost certain attack. The villages were too exposed, too easy to access, too easy to steal from without anyone noticing. At the same time, they were going into the forest more frequently—rescuing girls, engaging with militants, confiscating weapons. The president of Nigeria, Goodluck Jonathan, spoke boldly to the media about winning the battle against Boko Haram. He praised the bravery of the army and its dangerous search-and-destroy operations. But the hunters knew the truth. Soldiers could never win this war without the deep knowledge of the terrain that Bukar and the others had learned to navigate as young children. It was their forest, and it had been lost to Boko Haram. No presidential proclamation could change that. What of the hundreds of girls who'd been taken hostage? The hundreds—maybe thousands— of villagers who'd been slaughtered? Yes, many militants had been rooted out, but Boko Haram was always recruiting, always coercing young men to join up. Almost every day, it seemed another town or village was looted and overrun; women and girls suddenly disappeared, and men were forced to join or be killed. Any advances were only temporary. The militants always seemed to return stronger and more determined. But Bukar decided they would never be more determined than he was. And that would prove fatal.

Mai Ajirambe's death, his vicious murder, affected Aisha deeply. It was too close to their hunter's circle. He had been murdered for doing exactly what she and the others were doing: following government directives and protecting innocent Nigerians.

Now that Mai was gone, she made a vow to herself that she would exact revenge for his slaying. She would return the favour to those who had raised their bloodied machetes against his throat. And she knew exactly who the recipient would be.

Bula Yaga was a notorious commander even by the standards of Boko Haram. Moving in and out of his Sambisa sanctuary with impunity, he would raid a village or a farm, take what he needed, kill whomever he decided he wanted to kill, and return to the untouchable darkness of the forest. If you think of Boko Haram as an Islamist mafia, he was a capo or a don. And just as mafia reputations are built on brutality, Bula Yaga had reached an eminent status by being bloodthirsty. Aisha knew the man's ruthlessness almost as well as she knew the strengths and weaknesses of her own fellow hunters. Mai's beheading could only be his handiwork. Much like Bukar Jimeta, she was consumed by endless fury and a fierce determination to avenge his murder. Boko Haram, it sometimes seemed to Aisha, killed with impunity. How many of its commanders had been captured? Very few. How many had surrendered? Very few. Mostly they were killed without mercy, as they had killed. It was the order of vengeance: make those who'd caused such horrible suffering suffer horribly in return. But that was not considered to be acceptable behaviour in a modern country like Nigeria, one of Africa's richest nations.

"We must arrest these barbarians and put them on trial," said President Jonathan from the faraway safety of Abuja. Aisha did not argue with that, but she understood better than most how this war worked. She had heard stories of hunters committing extrajudicial killings, and they disturbed her. And there were other stories—horrible stories that some hunters were raping the girls they'd rescued from the forest. A treasonous violation that in Aisha's mind had to be punished with castration. A woman who grew up believing in the honour of hunters, she was guided by a sense of justice that went beyond loyalty to those around her. Yet she also knew the hunter's mindset and the predatory instinct that lurked under the surface. Still, such behaviour would undermine the entire government eradication campaign, hunters and soldiers working together to destroy Boko Haram. And how could anyone trust the Queen Hunter to be their protector if she was a part of such terrible things?

For all that, she still wanted to find Bula Yaga and subject him to the truest form of justice. The justice he deserved, not the justice upheld by people in high places far away from the forest and its secret barbarities.

Aisha was not a mother herself, and sometimes wondered if she would ever be one, but she could understand the fear of losing a child to Boko Haram. She tried to imagine a mother's agony as she wondered where her daughters were, what abuse they might be suffering.

She'd always thought she would have children, or at least one child. But it seemed her body had other plans. She had been married, briefly, years before, to a man from another village. He had wanted to have a family immediately, but it never happened. They both assumed Aisha was unable to conceive. After a year of trying, they quietly divorced. So instead of experiencing the joy of motherhood, she turned her attention to working with government forces, going into the forest, and rescuing many, many girls—so many she had lost count. With her team, she had also confiscated an untold number of Boko Haram's weapons, mostly military and police weapons, stolen from burned and ransacked villages and dead police officers.

Boko Haram fighters were tenacious and elusive. They despised the hunters as government stooges who, duped into battle against their own people, were unwilling to lay down their weapons and submit to a higher belief. For every girl who escaped their clutches in the forest, they would take two or three more as they continued to raid and raze villages through- out Borno and Adamawa States. They terrorized the countryside, scavenging for food and supplies, as well as new recruits. Some- times, the hunters had advance notice of these raids, from gov- ernment intelligence or rumours circulating around Maiduguri.

In July 2017, Aisha was in the forest on a different mission when Bukar and other members of the team got one such tip and loaded up their trucks with long guns and ammunition to drive south. They were bound for Dagu, which was tiny and would be easy to defend, thought their new commander. They drove through the afternoon, a Friday, arriving on the outskirts of the village around midnight, just after the militants did.

They drove into an ambush.

The shooting started within seconds. Residents were startled awake by the sound of rapid gunfire. Many escaped into the hills, dodging the firefight that swirled around them. The militants had arrived in the dark, dressed in police uniforms, with enough ammunition to raid several villages. They outnumbered the hunters, most of whom were left cowering behind their vehicles, unable to fire back with any accuracy.

The hunters wanted to retreat, but Bukar did not. He was firm in his belief that he had never lost a fight with Boko Haram, and he was determined not to lose this one. After running out of ammunition, the hunters scrambled into their trucks and sped away, leaving their commander on his own.

When the villagers left their hiding spots and returned to their razed homes the next morning, they found his body with an axe wound through the chest.

One of the hunters later said they called him Baka Ja Da Baya, or the man who never turns his back on his enemy. He fought on, the story went, until he was armed with only a hunting knife. When they couldn't kill him with a gun, they resorted to using an axe.

Aisha heard the news several hours later, as she was returning from the Sambisa. She knew it had to be Bula Yaga. Her nemesis had once again humiliated her small band of hunters and executed their leader.

The newspapers described the ambush in tragic tones: a great fighter felled at the hands of a notorious sadist who killed and tortured women and girls. More than ever, Aisha wanted to chase him to the ends of the forest and slit his throat. Yet this was a tragic and significant turning point in her life. With the old man and now Bukar gone, the others looked to her for leadership in the midst of tragedy. An unmarried Nigerian woman, a woman of the forest, treated not as an equal but as commander. The Queen Hunter.

Rumours soon emerged that Bula Yaga had finally been tracked down and killed during a military operation. But when pictures of a body appeared on social media, those who had met or fought against the furtive commander all agreed it was not his.

Word began to spread beyond Nigeria about a fierce huntress who led her band of men into the Sambisa, chasing down terrorists. It was a tantalizing story and a powerful counter to the memory of the girls of Chibok, torn away from their families and held as hostage brides. The fearless Aisha Bakari Gombi, armed with a long gun, dressed in green fatigues, pursuing men with a vicious resolve. Antelope hunter turned Boko Haram hunter. Tall, almost burly, yet silent as a night beast as she stalked her prey through the forest.

And journalists weren't the only ones taking an interest.

Muhammadu was a tall, gentle, and learned man who had grown up near the town of Gombi in Adamawa State. He had heard of this fearsome Queen Hunter living among them, and he was intrigued, if not infatuated. He saw her here and there, read about her, but never spoke to her. With all the attention she was getting, he wondered if he would ever have the chance. Nothing seemed to distract her from her mission; he found that mystifying. She was beguiling.

He saw her again in 2018, at the Salala, an annual festival where the hunters swore oaths to uphold the laws of nature. It was a day of rituals and socializing. The ceremony around the blessing of the guns was now more of an incantation for success in hunting Boko Haram than big game. Aisha gave a short speech on a hot and sunny afternoon, assuming her role with confidence. Muhammadu decided this was his chance. He listened intently and then, out of desperation and persistence, he penned a message asking her to meet him and had somebody slip it into her hand. Nothing happened. She didn't move. As he now tells the story, two more emissaries came back empty-handed. And then, unexpectedly, she was standing in front of him, surrounded by her battalion of hunters. He could feel the heat of their gaze on his face.

"Aisha Bakari," he said, "I am Muhammadu."

She looked straight into his eyes. "What do you want?"

"I want to speak to you. I want to ask you why you are not married. You are a beautiful woman. Why don't you have a partner?"

Aisha scoffed. "Who would want to marry someone like me? I'm not thinking about marriage."

This was not surprising to Muhammadu, but he wanted to challenge her.

"Why would you say that? Do you think men are afraid of you? Because I am not."

Aisha deepened her gaze. "Look at me," she said. "I am dirty and dusty and I go out to kill people. Who would marry me?"

That was the permission Muhammadu needed.

"Will you give me your phone number? I would like to get to know you more."

Aisha wasn't used to someone being so direct. Nor did she ever expect to have a suitor, given her age and itinerant lifestyle. But this man had kind eyes, and she smiled in spite of herself.

She didn't answer the first few times he called because she was in the forest. But he was persistent. He finally reached her when she came back to Gombi, and they started a conversation that lasted for several hours over several days. They then met and shared a meal, talking all the while about their lives and Aisha's mission. Muhammadu could see and feel the passion she had for hunting terrorists. The more time they spent together, the more Aisha relaxed around him. As a woman, not a hunter. She enjoyed his company, but more than that, she enjoyed having someone speak to her as an equal. She felt she could be completely open with Muhammadu and he wouldn't judge or question her decisions.

After a few months, he starting bringing up marriage. She recoiled at first, out of selfishness, unsure what effect it would have on her work. How would he feel about his wife going into the forest every few weeks, with the very real possibility she might not come back? She was already committed. It was easier to say no. But he made her smile, and the idea of sharing her life with this kind man became more appealing to her the more she turned it over in her head. He kept asking, until she finally relented.

Under Hausa custom, the groom and his family are obliged to meet the bride's parents to make a formal marriage request. Since Aisha's father was dead and her mother suffered from dementia, other relatives were called upon to give their blessing. A small bride price was agreed, and the *fatihah* was set for a few weeks later, in February 2019.

As they grew into marriage, working through the newness of it, Muhammadu took on his new role with immense pride and usefulness. He became her gatekeeper. She the hunter in demand, he the lion at the door. He greeted all callers with a firm regard, doing his best to protect her from anyone she didn't want to see. All were offered a cup of tea or water before being ushered in to see Aisha or shown to the door.

"More men should support their wives," he would tell visitors.

Most importantly, he applied no pressure for her to have a child. Aisha had warned Muhammadu before they got married that she likely couldn't have children, and she told him that if he wanted his own family, he should find someone else. But he didn't care. He was marrying for himself, for love, he told her, and if that meant he would not have children, then he would not have children.

They lived in a small compound with her ailing mother. It soon became a gathering place for Aisha's team. After Mai Aji-rambe's murder, armed hunters stood at the front gate, making sure all visitors were screened and keeping close watch on the road outside for militants daring to attack. Aisha still led her men into the forest, but like her husband, she had taken on a new role. She was now the team's mentor and spent most of her time training new recruits, many of them young women with ambitions to be like her.

What she hadn't counted on was the sudden realization of a child growing in her womb. It was difficult to grasp the magnitude of what was happening. How was this possible? She had given up on motherhood; her body had told her as much, but now it was changing and shifting and swelling with new life.

"It's a girl," she told her husband. "I just know. It's a girl." It seemed right that it would be, in the universe of a woman known as the Queen Hunter. "Alhamdulillah. *Mun gode Allah.*" Thanks be to God for this miracle.

Sa'adatu was an easy baby. She slept a lot at first and did not cry much. Aisha wanted her child to inherit strength from her and wisdom from Muhammadu. Both parents were surprised when she started to pull herself up very early on. Soon, she was crawling all over the compound. She was independent, brushing off other children's attempts to play with her. She would join in when she wanted, on her terms and with her dolls. She turned away from visitors who cooed and attempted to cuddle with her. But it was hard to blame them. Her big eyes and bubbling curiosity intrigued even the surliest of hunters. Muhammadu was always amused when Sa'adatu refused to oblige anyone who wanted to hold her. But he loved being able to take her back and explain that she already had a mind of her own. And Aisha felt a love she'd thought she would never experience. She also felt a deep gratitude for the miracle that was Sa'adatu. She could stare at this little creature all day, mesmerized by her smile, her every breath. And for the first time, she was gripped by a sense of fear. She finally understood the life-shattering anguish of all those mothers who'd been robbed of their girls by Boko Haram. Suddenly, her work had a new purpose.

The Queen Hunter, Aisha, with her daughter, Sa'wadatu, at her home in Yola. Her husband, Muhammadu, looks on.

12
SURRENDER

MAMA BOKO HARAM looked at the number that was calling on her mobile. She wasn't sure she recognized it, but she picked up anyway, hoping it was the call she had been waiting for. A few days had passed since she sent Nneka back into the Sambisa to try to convince her brother, one of Boko Haram's senior commanders, to surrender and bring out three of the remaining Chibok girls. She had heard nothing since.

"Yes, this is she," she said into the phone. She listened for a few seconds, then interrupted. "Where is he now and how long has he been there? Okay, I will see him. Later this afternoon and the place we discussed before. He's alone, I assume? Okay, good. See you later."

She put down the phone and turned to one of her aides, a man named Prince who looked after fundraising and outreach for her foundation. "It's not him," she said, referring to Nneka's brother. "It's someone else not as senior. But we should meet him anyway."

Prince, a tall man, thickly built, with a narrow moustache that made it look like he was perpetually smiling, said, "Of course." He handed her a file of papers to review and sign.

The foundation was headquartered in a set of buildings just off a main street in Maiduguri. Like many other buildings in this dust bowl of a city, these were hidden behind metal gates closely guarded by men with guns. The offices all opened onto a central courtyard where cars were parked. Mama's office was the largest. An air-conditioning unit made the room more comfortable in the heat of the season.

The door to Mama's office opened, and her daughter, Ummi, came in.

"Mama," she said, "I'm just dropping this off with you." She left a folder on her mother's desk.

"Where is my grandson?" Mama asked.

Ummi opened the door again, and a young woman carrying a small child walked in.

"Come here, come here, my grandson!" Mama's tone of voice changed completely. The tough negotiator in charge of winning the release of hostages had been replaced by a doting grandmother cooing at a child now bouncing on her knee.

"Mama, we have to go. Please let me know what you think." Ummi nodded at the folder she'd left on the desk. "We'll see you later."

Mama kissed the boy and handed him to her daughter.

"Okay, see you later."

She was reading the folder Ummi had left on the desk when her mobile rang again. She looked at the number and this time decided to ignore it.

Meeting a Boko Haram commander who had walked out of the Sambisa was not going to be easy and could very well be dangerous. The man, who went by Mustapha in the forest, was now hiding out at a relative's house and would have to find a way to meet Mama at her agreed spot in the railroad district without being discovered by government authorities. Mama had charged Prince with the job of getting him safely there and back. Her security people had gone ahead to make sure there were no surprises, and when they gave the all-clear later that afternoon, she hopped into the passenger side of one of the foundation's SUVs and motioned for the driver to start the vehicle. Prince was already seated in the back.

After a half hour through traffic and along bumpy roads, the car stopped in front of a shed. Mama got out, Prince following. There was already another vehicle there, a red SUV, and one of Mama's security people nodded in the direction of some trees in the distance. Hassan, the foundation's program director and one of her most trusted advisors, was also with them. He would be able to translate if Mustapha's Hausa was not strong enough. Mama didn't know enough Kanuri to carry on a conversation as vital as this on her own.

Mustapha was waiting underneath a neem tree, his face partly obscured by a branch. He stepped out from under it as Mama approached. He bowed toward her, and tentative greetings were exchanged.

"Salaam Alaikum."

"Salaam Alaikum."

A mat had been laid out under the tree so they could sit more comfortably in the shade. Mama slipped off her shoes and stared at the man, taking the measure of him. Mustapha was tall and had shorn hair, but his kameez did little to hide his thinness. Cheeks sunken and eyes yellowed, he looked nothing like one of Boko Haram's fearsome generals. In fact, she thought, he looked scared and exhausted.

"Please sit," Hassan said, in English for Mama and Kanuri for Mustapha.

Mama took her place across from the Boko Haram commander and studied him carefully. She knew why he had come out of the forest, but she wanted him to tell her.

No doubt, she thought to herself, it would be the same story she'd heard from many others of late.

"How long have you been in the forest with them?" She wanted to start at the beginning.

At first, his answers came slowly, one reluctant word at a time. His voice was flat and he spoke in a monotone. But nothing he said came as a surprise to her.

When Boko Haram militants had overrun his village nine years before, in 2010, they did what they do in every village— separate the men from the women. The men had a choice: join them or be killed. Which was no choice at all. Mustapha joined. The militants spent several weeks in the village at first, with him acting as a guard against those seeking to escape. But when rumours spread that the military was coming to take back the village, he left with the others to head into the forest. For all she knew, he had already started to kill.

In the forest, he rose through the ranks until he became a senior commander, the position from which he spoke to her now. She had no doubt he was guilty of committing many atrocities along the way.

"How many people did you have to kill?" She didn't mean to ask this aloud, but her voice had outrun her thoughts.

Mustapha shook his head. He didn't know how many. He had lost count over the years, he said. It made Mama wonder whether someone could lose his humanity. What part of his soul does a person lose when he takes the life of another?

He had no choice, Mustapha kept saying. It was kill or be killed. "If I'd tried to escape, they would have killed me. And I didn't really feel anything after a while, killing people. If anything, it was a good feeling. Good because the Qur'an had ordained it. The people were not following the Qur'an, so they had to be killed. If you do not follow the proper rules of Islam, you deserve to perish."

Mama, the Catholic turned Muslim, almost had to stifle a snort. But Mustapha was oblivious.

"The Qur'an orders it because if you do not follow what God has said, you are not of faith," he insisted. "The Qur'an has passed its judgement."

Mustapha's voice was flat. Mama couldn't tell if he truly believed what he was saying or was trying to justify his actions over the past nine years. Trying to rationalize the blood on his hands. Perhaps it was the only way he could live with himself— by dehumanizing the souls he had taken. If he could separate himself from his victims, were they really his victims at all?

"Why are you here now?" Again, Mama already knew the answer: Boko Haram had splintered, and if she understood correctly, the faction Mustapha was aligned with was going to lose influence because the other faction was attaching itself to the Islamic State, or IS. Many militants were losing their will to fight, confused about which faction to follow, and forest life was becoming more difficult.

Mustapha confirmed her theory. "I'm tired of this war. I am looking for peace."

Peace. Mama shook her head. She wondered if he was ready to face the consequences of his actions. Or was willing to submit to rehabilitation. She looked at him carefully, trying to decipher his real thoughts. Did he feel any regret or remorse for the pain he had caused? She didn't have to wonder long.

"I don't think about the people I had to kill. I have no feeling about it," he admitted. "I am just tired of the fighting. And there is no food in the forest. We are all starving."

"How many of you are there? And will you be able to convince others to leave?" Mama had already moved on from him. She wanted to know whether it would be possible to engineer a mass surrender.

"*Inshallah*. I think there are about three hundred, some children. They are all ready to come out. But in groups, not all at once. I can bring you twenty or thirty at a time."

"You bring them to me." Mama was firm.

"Yes, Mama, I will bring them to you. I feel very much better having talked to you. It feels good to come to you and ask for this help."

Mustapha then spoke rapidly to Hassan, almost too quickly

for him to be able to translate. When he was finished, Hassan turned to Mama.

"He says you are like a mother to them. Anything you tell him, he will accept. They didn't want to do this before because they were afraid that if the government got involved, they would be killed. They know you will not let this happen. What they have said before and what you have said before—all they have understood, now they are under your jurisdiction."

Mama looked at Mustapha. He wasn't one of her original sons, but here he was, a Boko Haram fighter, calling her Mama. It was a huge responsibility to ensure he would be safe from government retribution if he did surrender, and an even bigger one to make sure he would be successfully rehabilitated.

Mama needed insurance.

"They have to show me they are ready for peace," she said. And then, looking directly at Mustapha, she repeated: "You have to show me that you are ready for peace, ready to lay down your guns. It is one thing to say you want to come out, but you need to prove it to me. So go back to the forest and make a video. Send it to me. I want to see everyone who is ready to surrender to me. Otherwise, if you come out with your guns, they will kill you. The government will kill you. The video will be your peace symbol. Forward it to me immediately, and then I will know you are serious and I can make plans to help you leave the forest."

She also knew she needed time to figure out how she would house and rehabilitate these people, if they were all ready to come out. Hassan relayed this in Kanuri to Mustapha, who nodded but seemed confused by what Mama was asking. She interrupted.

"Tell him not to be afraid now. There is nothing to be afraid of with me. The government has my back. Security forces will not do anything if he comes to me. There will not be a scratch on him. Not a scratch."

Mustapha seemed satisfied with this. He promised to go back and send the video, then await further instructions from Mama. But his brow furrowed as he remembered the one thing he had to bring back to the forest. He bent his head to Hassan's ear, as if not wanting to be heard. Hassan listened for a few moments, nodding, and when Mustapha was finished, he spoke.

"He says he promised to bring them back some food and supplies from the city. So, Mama, if you can give him a hundred thousand naira, he can go to the market and buy what they need, then go back to the forest and give them the food they need. And then he can keep his word to them, and they will keep their word to you."

Mama thought about this. One hundred thousand naira was a few hundred US dollars, not an insignificant amount. And it proved to her again how desperate they were becoming in the forest. She had heard many stories of fighters quitting the insurgency because they were literally starving. The government and the military were constantly putting out press releases about how much territory they were taking back, but the truth was that much of the time, they didn't have to battle the depleted militants at all.

As Mama considered Mustapha's request, she felt a twinge of something. Was it pity? Sympathy? Because she saw all these men as her sons, it was hard to feel too much anger toward Mustapha, even though he showed no remorse. He looked in his fifties, but in reality, he was most likely in his mid-thirties. Worn. Tired. Old. That's what a decade of fighting and killing will do.

Mustapha would not meet her eyes. He had made his request. If he didn't return to the forest with food and other provisions, he would lose some of the influence needed to bring the others out. This was about proving to them that he had credibility with Mama.

"Let me think about it and I will talk to you later," she finally said. "Mama is tired now." This was a calculated lie. She had already decided she would give him the money, but she wanted him to wait for it. She motioned to Hassan. "Drive him back to the city, and we will be in touch with him in a while."

In Kanuri, Hassan explained to Mustapha that he would be taken back to his relative's house, and they would be in touch later in the day or the next day. The commander nodded. He was in no hurry to get back to the forest anyway, especially if he was going to return empty-handed. He said something in Kanuri to Hassan, who translated for Mama.

"He says he is very happy and thankful to have been able to meet with you and talk to you. Whatever Mama wants, he will do. He feels very good to be here and to see Mama. And he will keep his word. He thanks you, Mama."

Mama smiled at him. "Thank you."

The meeting was over. Mama's security detail did a quick sweep around the area. They had been so focused on the meeting underneath the neem tree that they didn't notice a small group had gathered where they left their vehicles. They motioned for her to wait until they were satisfied that it was safe to leave. She watched as they approached the group and had a few words.

After several minutes, they signalled the all-clear. Mustapha was now standing up and speaking quietly with Hassan in Kanuri. He towered over Mama, who was standing next to both of them, trying without much luck to understand the conversation. One of the men stepped forward and motioned for Mustapha to follow him.

"Thank you, Mama." He bowed his head to her before being led to the back of the red SUV.

"Let them leave first," she said, scanning the area herself. She wanted to make sure no one followed the red vehicle. She was always worried that the authorities were tracking her to get to her boys. If Mustapha were arrested, it would send the wrong message to the hundreds of others in the forest who might also want to surrender. He would have to get back to the encampment without attracting too much attention, which is why Mama had hesitated to give him money to buy food and other provisions. But she knew she could not refuse his request in the end. She directed Prince to get the cash to him the next day, and to make sure he understood that he had to send the video to her as soon as he got back to the forest. She needed to know how many people she was dealing with, and whether they were serious about leaving Boko Haram.

Still, she was waiting for the big surrender: Nneka's brother. He would bring three Chibok girls with him, and eventually, the remaining Chibok girls would be released. That would be a huge coup for her and her foundation. From the beginning, the government had bungled everything to do with the Chibok situation. Even though more than a hundred girls had been released and were now being schooled and housed in a secure location in Abuja, that left at least another hundred still in the forest, more than six years after they were taken. Even their parents were losing hope that they would be found. Some had no doubt been indoctrinated into Boko Haram and would never leave the Sambisa. But there was always a chance that others were still alive and being held against their will. And if Mama could secure their release, the government would have no choice but to work with her and help fund the Complete Care and Aid Foundation's efforts to rehabilitate them.

She looked at her phone to see if there was a missed call. There wasn't. Nneka had promised to call once she'd spoken with her brother. Perhaps it had taken her longer to make the trip back into the forest. Or perhaps he had moved camps. What if something had happened to her along the way?

Just as she was starting to get carried away, Prince broke her thoughts by asking how much money he should take to Mustapha.

"Give him what he asked for," she said. It was part of the deal. She would keep her word and he would be forced to keep his.

If this was actually going to happen, Mama had to think hard and work fast. There was a good chance the men would be arrested if they came out in big numbers. She would have to make arrangements to house them somewhere. She also knew that the authorities would figure out very quickly what she was doing, so it was in her best interests to reach out to them. But here was the tricky part: she was engineering a surrender they could not, and if they felt that she was somehow helping to tamp down the insurgency in a way they had not been able to, they could undermine her as they had before, by killing the men when they emerged. It was a bit like walking a tightrope, and she was too apolitical to have much patience for pandering to the government. She was Mama Boko Haram, after all, and she had insight and influence that the authorities could have exploited, had they been willing to work with her from the beginning. Instead, they seemed too eager to pursue military options and push the rhetoric of crushing the insurgency. It was almost counterproductive. How can you convince the militants to surrender if they think you're going to kill them when they do?

Still, she took comfort in the fact that she wasn't going to have to do this alone. She had enough connections in Nigeria and abroad, with different NGOs and security companies, to help with getting the men out and finding them safe housing, far away from the handcuffs of authorities. She had the support; she just needed to work out the logistics. And that would mean reaching out to some of her contacts in Abuja. Mama accepted that she would have to continue massaging politicians' egos to ensure that her foundation could carry on the vital work of rehabilitating extremists and slowly bringing the insurgency to an end.

"We'll have to brainstorm," she said out loud as she watched the red vehicle carrying Mustapha weave through the busy Maiduguri traffic.

PART III: RECKONING

13
UNDER THE NEEM TREE

GAMBO, ASMA'U, AND ZARA arrived in Maiduguri together. It was morning in early May 2019, and the heat of summer was already starting to build. Over the past several years, the girls had gotten to know each other through Asma'u and Gambo's cousin Ibrahim and his friend Kabir, a journalist based out of Yola who had been reporting on the Boko Haram insurgency from the beginning. Ibrahim acted like the girls' guardian, and he thought it would be good for them to spend more time together, given their shared experience, and to get to know other girls like Zara, who had also escaped the Sambisa. They shared their stories with Kabir, as well as with the foreign journalists he sometimes shepherded through the region. Interest from international media organizations skyrocketed after the Chibok kidnapping in 2014, and ever since, there had been a semi-steady stream of reporters parachuting into northeastern Nigeria. But it was often difficult to interest them in stories that weren't connected to the Chibok girls. They were the hashtag, the headline.

The three young women relished the time they got to spend together. Gambo and Asma'u had become like aunties to little Aisha, whom Zara brought along every time the three of them met. On this trip, they'd come to Maiduguri to visit a rehabilitation centre for girls who had managed to escape Boko Haram. Zara had long heard about "mind doctors"—psychologists—who were working with girls like them, and she thought they might help her as well. Asma'u was curious. Gambo was more skeptical. She thought there might be better ways to channel her anger, which had only been festering since she'd fled the forest.

When they arrived at the gates of a large complex in the city, they hesitated just a little, suddenly unsure about why they were there. It felt like a big, uncertain step. But any doubts were erased when the gate opened and they were ushered into the main building. They were greeted by a woman with a broad smile and gentle eyes.

"*Sannu*," she said, looking at each of them in turn. "Welcome. Please come in."

Dr. Fatima Akilu had wanted to be a writer. As a Nigerian teenager in a boarding school in Kent, England, she was a prolific poet, and she later managed to convince her mother to allow her to study in the United States. Fatima settled in California, thinking she would study English. Instead, she became obsessed with serial killers. This was around the time of the Golden State Killer, who terrorized California in the late 1970s and 1980s with dozens of rapes and murders. She couldn't read enough about the case and others like it, including that of the Green River Killer, two states away in Washington. It both confounded and amazed her that someone could get away with killing so many people and be able to elude authorities for so long. She devoured everything she could get her hands on about the cases—interviews with investigators, profilers, even the devastated families of the victims. What makes someone a serial killer? Is there something different about their psychology? What causes someone to kill again and again?

In college, she joined a sorority, and as part of her community service, she spent time at a juvenile detention hall outside of Los Angeles, where she had a chance to observe people who'd committed the most heinous crimes. She started working with a girl who was barely sixteen, just a couple of years younger than Fatima herself. The girl and her boyfriend had allegedly killed a man while on holiday in Mexico, then dismembered him and dumped his body parts one at a time on a road trip back to California. Fatima was astounded that the girl seemed to show almost no remorse for what she had done. She needed to understand why. She realized that she would have to major in both English and psychology.

In the summers, she spent time at Saint Elizabeths, a major psychiatric hospital in Washington, DC, studying and working with people who had been admitted because of violent tendencies. She probed, analyzed, and explored every case she was able to access.

Years later, she would put those experiences and her training to use in her native Nigeria. The Boko Haram insurgency was creating victims and radicals at an alarming rate, and the government seemed to have no plan for how to heal those who wanted to leave or had managed to escape. But when Fatima first returned to the country, she had a difficult time finding a job as a psychologist. People didn't understand the concept of mental health. "People's idea of mental health," she explained, "was only what you would require in-patient treatment for in a psychiatric hospital. That was their total understanding of mental health."

Eventually, she and her sister founded the Neem Foundation, an NGO focused on treating the trauma that was threatening a generation of Nigerians. The need was immeasurable, and the government was incapable of providing any services for the mental health crisis the insurgency had created. At the same time, foreign NGOs working in northeastern Nigeria were focused on humanitarian needs. The conflict had also displaced hundreds of thousands in the region, so food, shelter, and safety were obviously top of mind. No one was thinking about the psychological impact of trauma. But Fatima knew that if it was not addressed, it would become intergenerational—a cycle of pain that would be passed down for decades to come.

A few days before Zara, Gambo, and Asma'u visited, Fatima was at Neem's rehabilitation facility and school in Maiduguri. Set behind a heavy gate in a nondescript neighbourhood, Lafiya Sariri was a sanctuary for those who'd escaped the Sambisa.

"*Sannu*, Dr. Akilu!" Fatima was greeted by a chorus of girls, smiles spread across their faces, all looking up at her.

"*Sannu! Sannu!*"

She had interrupted their reading class, but now they gave her their undivided attention. Everyone had the chance to greet her, and they were eager and animated.

"We can accommodate only a hundred or so here," she explained later, almost apologetically. "It's so that we can give them the support they require to be able to reintegrate into the community." She said she found out early on that survivors of Boko Haram, while not unlike other survivors of sexual abuse, were also witnesses to horrific violence. The trauma inflicted on them impacted how they responded to the different stimuli she and her team of specialists put forward. Years earlier, during one of her initial assessments for the government, she and several other psychologists were brought in to evaluate several hundred girls of all ages who had been released by the terror group. For the first few days, there was simply silence. No amount of prodding elicited a response. Then the psychologists brought in toys to try to see whether that might help the survivors, especially the younger ones, open up. Instead, the girls destroyed all the toys. They ripped the heads off the dolls and stomped all over everything else. Subsequent therapy sessions revealed that they had been conditioned in the forest not to utter a sound for fear of being beaten or killed by their captors. Toys were also *haram*, so destroying them meant that you adhered to Boko Haram's beliefs and would be spared from torture or worse.

In 2012, after that initial assessment, Goodluck Jonathan's government asked Fatima to develop a rehabilitation program for former members of Boko Haram, to help them leave the insurgency and reintegrate into society. It was a near impossible task, but she got to work, looking for support and cultivating relationships in the community.

Looking back years later, she acknowledged what a serious challenge that turned out to be. "That was the hardest part. I think it's hard for communities as a whole, and don't forget, we don't just work with girls—we also work with boys and young men—and that's why the community work is so complicated. It takes a long time to convince communities to accept the idea of rehabilitation . . . because why should they accept people who have caused them so much anguish? Destroyed their lives, killed family members? We have a lot of people coming back who have killed their fathers, or who have killed their mothers and family members on their journey into Boko Haram. And to ask the remaining family members to forgive them—it's asking a lot. But we also, as a society, know that they have nowhere to go. I mean, we're not going to create alternative societies where we have people who have joined terrorist groups living in these enclaves. I've seen it in Colombia and other countries, and I don't think it works . . . The best possible outcome for us, I think, at the moment as a country, is to find a way to reconnect, to forgive, to be reunited."

She recalled a story about one of the imams she helped to rehabilitate. He was, in fact, Boko Haram's chief imam at the time. He had been captured and was in prison. Initially, he didn't want to speak with her. She knew it would do no good to put him into the deradicalization part of the program straight away, so she decided she would take the time to get to know him and gain his trust. As a Muslim herself, she could speak to him about the Qur'an and ask questions about his interpretation of it in a non-threatening, almost curious way. After about a year, he was ready to take part in the program proper. And he remains one of her proudest deradicalization accomplishments.

"He came to me after and asked us to help educate his children. He said that I had helped open his eyes. He called himself a blind man leading people into a hole. It was a complete turnaround for him, someone who had believed so fervently that Western education was not Islamic. But that turnaround came with trauma, because then he started wondering whether God [would] ever forgive him for all the horrible things he did and led others into doing. So we had to work through that with him. And after all of it, when he was released from prison, he decided to enrol himself in school."

Fatima paid for the family's school fees because she wanted to do something to keep him on the path away from extremism. She remains certain that education is the only prevention—and cure—for terrorism.

But just a little more than two years into her mandate, Fatima was unceremoniously dismissed. In May 2015, Goodluck Jonathan was swept out of office by a former general, Muhammadu Buhari, on a wave of promises to crush the insurgency. The innovative program that she had developed and tailored specifically for Boko Haram insurgents was in danger of being swept aside as well. Threats, not therapy, were the order of the day. In Buhari's government, there would be no "soft" approach to the terrorists, especially because Boko Haram's violence was reaching its peak. The Chibok girls had been taken the year before, and there was still no progress in the effort to find them and hold the men who had taken them to account. Meanwhile, the group was stepping up its attacks through the region and even targeting the capital, Abuja. People were frustrated by what seemed like an inadequate government response, so they had voted for a strongman. Buhari waited barely a few months before replacing Fatima with a colonel no one had heard of before.

It could have been soul-crushing, but it simply made her more determined to continue doing the work she believed in. Two years later, Neem was born.

Now, at her rehabilitation facility, the sum of those experiences was being put to good use. Fatima's philosophy of rehabilitation is both learned and studied. Carrot, not stick. Sow trust, not fear. But the sheer scale of the task as the insurgency continued to create both victims and extremists was daunting, so she reached out to communities she hoped would be willing to host them. It would sometimes take years for a village to allow former Boko Haram members in. There was one particular incident that still pains her to speak about. She and her team had worked with a community for months, preparing it to accept some fighters into a rehabilitation facility on the outskirts of the town. When the men came out of the forest, community elders summarily executed them all. Fatima still shudders at the horror and guilt she felt. Trust, she realized, would take much longer to build. Another village agreed to take some men back, but only if they were forced to live across the river from the town itself, ostracized from the rest of the villagers. It was draining, soul-wrenching work, requiring intense counselling on both sides. But it was the only way forward.

Meanwhile, what about their victims? What of the thousands of young girls who had been tormented and abused to near insanity? What treatment would bring them back from the nightmares, the memories, and the cruel alienation they suffered afterward? Many who had escaped or been rescued by the Civilian Joint Task Force remained isolated in remote communities and villages. What chance did they have of rehabilitation there? It wasn't possible for them to travel to Maiduguri for trauma counselling, so Fatima decided that the counselling would have to travel to them.

One of Neem's first programs was a revolutionary idea called Counselling on Wheels. A combination of peacebuilding and therapy, it led to extensive consultation with local officials, including tribal elders and government representatives, in a push to make their participation a centrepiece of the program. Without that kind of sustainable relationship, it would never have worked. Fatima made the same pitch to potential donors. Therapy was expensive, and the government in Abuja didn't have the budget for it, at least not at the scale required.

"We have a community liaison officer, and he goes out and he assesses different communities and finds out what the needs of those communities are, the levels of people who have been displaced within those communities, [the numbers of] people who are traumatized. And then he has a week-long session of dialogues with the community to help them understand what mental health is. What is trauma? What does it look like? What kind of help would Neem provide? What would that help look like? So then we come in the second week, and usually by then there is a waiting list for our services. But we don't go in blind because a lot of people will tell us: 'When you first came, we didn't know what you were offering us. Most people come—they offer food, they offer clothing, they offer medical services. So what exactly are you? You're just talking to us.' But after they've been with us a couple of weeks, they say: 'Well, we're now able to sleep. I don't have that pounding in my chest as much. And I'm able to take care of my child.' So they begin to understand the value of the therapy."

The program quickly attracted international media attention, and Neem earned a reputation for innovation in treating survivors of gender-based and other types of violence perpetrated by extremist groups. But Fatima demurred when given credit for the progress made by her foundation since it started working in the region. Instead, she pointed to the work of some other NGOs, calling their efforts "life-changing." Still, she said, all the work that's being done is not enough because the numbers are staggering.

"So whatever Neem is doing is just a drop in the bucket. It's pretty insignificant compared to the needs. We need a better, coordinated government response. I think NGOs do an amazing job—I've seen some really dedicated NGOs that have transformed people's lives—but the reality is that NGOs cannot do scale, and we must accept that only the government has the resources, the way to mobilize and to have a response where everybody that needs services has access to those services. Only the government can do that. Our job now is to provide models and examples of what can be done, and to push government to become more involved in this area."

So far, she added wearily, she's seen no evidence of the political will to be more engaged.

A Neem community outreach workshop in Maiduguri.

The rehabilitation centre in Maiduguri was designed as a place of order, comfort, and discovery. A place for girls to re-engage with their education and deal with their trauma at the same time.

Fatima caught up with the staff and checked in with the students, offering a sympathetic ear to some and an encouraging word to others. In the computer lab, faces stared at screens. Some students were reading; others were doing schoolwork. At least one was mesmerized by a game, her screen full of multi-coloured shapes. The adult in the room was happy to let the girls do whatever they wanted. Around the corner from the main building, past an open area where a raucous volleyball game was in progress, there was a standalone structure about the size of two trailers. Inside was a long wooden communal table around which a dozen girls were seated. No one spoke. The silence was punctuated only by the sound of pencils at work, the occasional shuffling of paper, and the gentle whir of a fan. Large paintings adorned the spaces between windows. Two easels sat in one corner, waiting for their charges. But for now, the girls had bowed their heads and were focused on their drawings. Once in a while, one would look up to assess a friend's drawing or pick up a different coloured pencil. Light streamed in through the slits in the thatched window coverings, illuminating the works in progress.

Art therapy gave these girls a different avenue to express themselves. They were free to say what they wanted, without having to use words. Visitors were often surprised by how violent some of the images were: guns pointed at the heads of faceless figures; bodies, big and small, lying on the ground; red for blood, black for death; angry scribbles with thicker colours. It was hard to think that this beautiful, calm, and light-filled space could inspire such dark thoughts, such dark imagery.

Chika Bukar, the head teacher, walked around the room, silently observing. She knew this was just one way for the girls to tell her and their counsellors what was haunting them. Music, sports, and drama were all part of the curriculum. Some girls were more expressive in sports, which allowed their aggression an outlet. Others danced their way out of their sadness. Still others were better able to write about their feelings.

"Some of the things they have seen," Chika said, "are horrific. Some of them have watched their loved ones killed in front of them. Some of them had their loved ones abducted. Some of them, it is their communities that have been attacked. So they are here with multiple traumas. Some come to school crying, and at times we see others moody. Some of them, when they first came on board here, they were very, very aggressive. With our tools and methods, we have been able to help them open up, and we've been able to give them the self-esteem and confidence that will help them cope. It's part of the support that we give to them—they have individual counselling but group counselling as well, and these extracurricular activities are part of that group therapy."

The girls occasionally looked up at Chika, moving their elbows so she could see their work. A drawing of a house with a family under its roof; a yellow duck with a large orange beak; a stand of trees. She nodded approvingly at them all, making small suggestions here and there, but generally left them to their own imaginations, their own memories.

These girls had come a long way from their first days at the Lafiya Sariri centre. Chika remembers the trauma they brought with them—so deep that they could not speak for days. Others came with an anger that made it seem impossible for anyone to reach them. But slowly, with therapy and patience and hard work, they started coming back from that dark and distant place.

At the end of the session, the girls put their pencils back in their cases and took their drawings, their meditations, with them to the next class.

14
COUNSELLING

THE AIR IN the room was damp and hot. Suffocating. The mugginess a harbinger of the rainy season to come. The wetter the air, the heavier the much-needed rains would be when they finally arrived. But there was something else, another weight that hung over those gathered, a common burden they had tried so hard to exorcise.

Gambo, Zara, and Asma'u were about to come face to face with the horrors they had tried so desperately to suppress. In front of them sat Maryam, Hassana, and Falmata. They were wearing slate-grey headscarves to match their slacks and bright orange tunics patterned with big blue daisies, the uniform of Lafiya Sariri.

Gambo, Zara, and Asma'u had come to the rehabilitation centre to see what recovery might look like, and what work they needed to do to get there. They found themselves sitting in a circle with their uniformed counterparts, a psychologist and two counsellors looking on. Zara's two-year-old toddler was with them as well, and the little girl wandered from one person to another, bewildered yet at home, somehow sensing that her mother was in a safe place.

"*Sannu*," said Fatima, or Dr. Akilu, as the girls knew her. *She is a beautiful woman*, Zara thought, with her welcoming smile, her hair wrapped up in a *gele* of the same red-and-white-checked fabric as her wrapper, a white shawl clinging to her shoulders, a wrinkle of concern furrowing her brow. She nodded at the three girls in uniform. Hassana and Falmata were seated next to each other. Maryam was seated between Gambo and Asma'u.

"We are here today because there are some girls visiting," Dr. Akilu said as she smiled at each one and nodded at the counsellors. "They have also suffered at the hands of Boko Haram, and they have come to talk to you so they do not feel so alone with the same problems. Because of the help you are getting and the counselling you are receiving from Peter and Laraba, you are stronger. And you give them hope of a brighter future, despite what you have all gone through."

She looked at the girls not in uniform. "Please feel free to ask them any questions," she said kindly. "Learn from their experiences and have faith that things will get better for you."

The girls murmured and nodded. Peter, the head counsellor, took the lead. "Maryam, Hassana, and Falmata—they have been through a lot. But they are doing better now. So feel free to share your experiences. This is a safe place to talk about things."

The girls looked at each other. Silence hung in their cautious glances.

Laraba prodded them gently. "Whatever is bothering us in our hearts, we should feel free to say it out loud here. Why don't we start by introducing ourselves?"

That seemed to break the ice, and the girls went around the room, exchanging names and shy smiles. Zara Isa. Gambo Musa. Asma'u Adamu. Hassana Sa'idu. Maryam Musa. Falmata Mohammed.

They sat stiffly. Hassana's arms were crossed over her chest. Falmata twirled her fingers. Asma'u looked from one girl to the next.

Laraba, the counsellor, cleared her throat. "We don't have to be afraid to ask each other things. Because in this way, we can strengthen one another, we can advise each other, encourage each other, and give each other strength. So you may think you are strangers now, but we are like a family whose members have come from other places. They have suffered like you. They face different challenges. May God reveal our innermost thoughts and concerns to us. Let us not hide anything that concerns us. Let's be open to each other."

The girls were still silent, unsure of the next steps.

"Falmata, why don't you start by telling us your story?" Laraba suggested. "We all have a story to tell, and once we tell each other, we will see we are not alone."

Falmata straightened her skirt with her palms, rubbing them against the fabric several times. She looked around the room and took a deep breath. Her voice started barely above a whisper.

"It was the first of September in 2014 when Boko Haram attacked our city. They came just after morning prayers into our town of Bama. They held us hostage; we could not go out of our homes. It was a Monday, just after morning prayers. They started shooting, and we were trapped. Then the men said they would go out. But anyone who dared go outside was killed. Slaughtered. They fired shots everywhere, just to announce they were there."

She paused and shuddered at the memory.

"Then, around three o'clock, they started shooting. They were shooting at us from the other side of a little river in town. Boko Haram had arrived, and the men were being killed. Soldiers who were supposed to be protecting us suddenly fled. Women were being taken, abducted. Boko Haram fighters kept coming into the town; they were being dropped off in vehicles. Everyone was being robbed. Black, white—everybody was robbed. They came in riding a motorcycle—two men on a motorbike armed with guns and bullets. This went on for two days. Then on Wednesday, we heard planes flying overhead, and [the government] started dropping bombs. It was so loud and I was so scared. My father learned that our neighbours had been killed. My mother was worried they would kill him, too, because they were killing all the men, so she told him to get into the ceiling. He went into the ceiling and spent the day inside, in the attic. When he came down, it was late at night. We could no longer tell time. But the bombs were still falling everywhere. The bombs chased Boko Haram from our town. Some soldiers ran into the river and into the forest. The planes just kept dropping bombs.

"The next day, the bombing continued. One exploded close to us and our house shook, and when I looked around, my mother was lying on the floor. She wasn't moving. I thought she was dead, so we all started shouting. Me and my two younger brothers, shouting at her and crying, afraid to go closer in case she was really dead.

"Finally our father said: 'Be silent! Let us check.' I was told to go and fetch cold water. I went to fetch water. I brought some water and poured it on her. She took a long breath. My father placed his ear on my mother's heart. Then she took a deep breath and got up. When she got up, our father said, 'Tomorrow morning, we will leave. Are you fit enough? We'll go out. God will grant us peace.'"

Little Aisha started to cry. Zara picked her up and bounced her on her knee. Laraba reached into her purse and pulled out a lollipop, unwrapped it, and gave it to the girl. She nodded at Falmata to continue.

"That evening, my mother went to give the imams some money and prayer items, an offering to God to help guide us through in peace. And then we prayed. The next morning, we left the house around eight. We took some water, that was all. We started walking. There were men everywhere with guns, but we kept going. We crossed the river and we never looked back. We passed through three other towns. But at this same time, Boko Haram soldiers were starting to take people back. Then my father said, 'Let's go down this road. I know someone who lives down this road; he is a friend of mine.' He said we [would] stop at the university entrance. And then my mother said, 'How can this road be the entrance to the university? Let's just follow this path. As long as it leads to somewhere that is safe from Boko Haram.' My father was certain. He insisted on going down the path he spied. So we followed the path. It was night. We were tired and wanted to sleep, but my father said no, we must continue.

"And so we went on till daybreak and rested along the way. And in the morning, we went to a town called Kashemir. And when we came to Kashemir, we were stopped by two men on a bicycle holding a gun. They said, 'Where are you going? There is no use trying to flee. Wherever you go, we are there.' They said to my father, 'Are you a public servant?' And then my father said, 'No, I'm not a professional. I'm not working.' He was asked, 'What is your business?' He said, 'I only buy goats. I trade in the market. I am just a trader.' That's when they searched my father—patted down his body and looked into his pockets. They saw a receipt. They said, 'What is this?' 'It's my business,' my father said. 'I bring goods to sell. They are names of those that I owe. It was in writing. And this is the list of my business partners.'

"Then my father asked for a drink. My mother gave it to him. After he drank, they took him away. They said if I refused to marry them, my mother and father and my little brothers [would] be killed. And we [would] be led away and would belong to them. Everyone was crying. My father was to be killed! I kept saying to them, 'You are going to kill people. You have no faith. This is not happening!' We were all crying. Our mother was begging them. They wouldn't listen. They leaned against my father and they were about to kill him. But then they were told to wait for their leader to come. My father called all of us, with his hands bound. He prayed for us. 'May God bless you all. God has given you the power to survive in a good world.'

"He was shaking his head. It touched me. His hands were bound. He kept saying, 'May God bless you all.' He said to my mother, 'Take care of my daughter and my children. And please give them a good life. Let them study. If you get outside, tell my mother, ask her to forgive me. And if you find another husband, you should marry again. I tell you . . . I strongly urge you to marry. Please look after my children. No matter how hard it might be, please live with my children. Wherever you go, let my children go too. Follow them and go with them.' And then, as he was talking to my mother, they came and said, 'Bring a gun.'"

Falmata stopped and shut her eyes, the memory so vivid she could see it happening all over again. And with her eyes still closed, she continued.

"'Stand up!' they ordered him. And then they dragged him, all the time yelling at him. 'Since you are not a pagan today, do you now accept Islam? Unless you find it difficult to convert since you have not converted to Islam?'

"My father said, 'I am not a pagan. Nor am I of Islam. It's not hard to see. It's my turn. You see this danger. If you kill me, it's Friday today, this water touches me, as the teachers have said, I accept my fate.' That was all he said. They were taking him away from us to kill him. I couldn't stand it any longer, so I ran after them and put my arms around my father. I was crying, telling them to stop.

"Then one of the Boko Haram soldiers came up to me and said, 'You're crazy!' I grabbed him. He dropped his gun, and with the other hand, he took a whip and whipped me. He kept whipping me, but I didn't let go. It was burning all over . . . My mother got up and fell; she got up and fell again. Turning, she said, 'Let my husband [go] free and let us go with my kids. Please tell them to stop.' Then the leader told them to leave me. I was ordered to lie down. If I got up, I would be shot. I cursed them. I kept saying: 'God is enough between you and us. In the hereafter, we will all have to answer to God.'

"So they said, 'Why don't you keep quiet, little girl?' The gun was loaded and shot in the air. I was still on the ground. My father was then taken to the side of the town. He was tied up and dragged, and later he was killed. They slaughtered everyone. Someone had cut me with a knife—I don't even know where, but my blood was flowing. The area was full of blood. The men said to us, 'Yes, your brother's blood is sprinkled upon you.' We told them, 'Our blood is sprinkled everywhere.' My mother was crying, saying, 'Just let me be killed before my children are taken away.' They said, 'You are ours too. You are already our wife. We cannot kill our wives because we love you.' She did not answer them; she refused to look at them. It was then we were taken away. We were taken to Sambisa. We [had] become theirs."

Around Falmata, the other girls were wiping their eyes with their hands and muffling their sobs so as not to interrupt her stream of memory. Asma'u blew her nose, thinking of her missing father and how close Falmata's experience mirrored her own. The girls caught each other's eyes and saw the same reflection.

"Go on," Laraba said gently.

Falmata nodded. Her voice, which had started so softly, gained a little strength and a few decibels. "In the forest, there was no food available. They won't bring you any food; you have to go looking. But you are also asked to stay at home. It was a no-win situation. Some other women who were there shared their food with us and with the other women whose children were crying.

"You do not dare run away from [the men]. If you run out, they will arrest you. If you go out the door, they will say, 'What, you want to get married? Or do you prefer to go to a pagan city?' We stayed there for close to four months. Their security eyes watch your every move."

She stopped again and took an audible breath. The other girls were entranced by her story. Falmata squeezed her eyes shut for a second and then opened them.

"That last night we heard gunshots," she continued. "My mother told us, 'Tomorrow morning, we will go back to Bama. Otherwise, we will certainly die here.' In the morning, we left before seven, never looking behind. We just kept walking and walking. We were getting hungry, and on the way, we passed by mango trees. We picked the fruit and ate until our stomachs were full. Then we went to look for water to take with us, but that was not as easy. It didn't matter; I was just happy to be leaving that place.

"As we walked, we headed up to the river. When we climbed on the hill, I looked down at the river—it was red. It was red with blood, and there were dead bodies floating and the corpses were swollen. They didn't look human. Blood and bodies and parts of bodies. I couldn't let my mind think about it too much. I just had to look away and get through it. My brothers did not see the blood. They walked in the river, in the bloody water, and they didn't even know it was blood until later. There was blood everywhere. When we got to a village on the way to Bama, Boko Haram was in the town. It was now theirs. They kept the weapons ready. Ready to kill and kill. They needed replacements for fighters who were tired and who wanted to leave. We kept going. We continued on that road for eleven days. No food or drink. Not even any milk for my littlest brother.

"We crossed the river. And after eleven days, we reached Bama. We saw my grandmother. She was in a wheelchair. My cousins were around her, and my mother went to her. She was crying. My mother is everything to us. We found out that my older cousins had been killed. Some were killed by bombs. Others had accidents. Others hid in the mosque. One was in the market when the bomb exploded. When we arrived here, everyone was watching us. After reaching Bama police station, people started to welcome us home. We greeted everyone—*sannu, sannu*—and we made our way along the road that led to our house. When we got there, the house was still there. It survived. We survived. And finally, I am back in my father's house."

Falmata was finished. She stared straight ahead, seemingly unaware that her story had brought the others to tears. After a long silence interrupted only by muffled sobs, Zara was the first to speak.

"Our greatest sympathies to you, Falmata. God is great."

Gambo nodded and then whispered, "May God grant you peace."

Laraba and Peter surveyed the room, making mental notes of the girls' reactions. Being able to speak about trauma is an important part of the healing process. They knew that the girls they had been working with at Lafiya Sariri were ready, but they were slightly worried about the new arrivals. Falmata smiled at Laraba, as if she knew what her counsellor was thinking.

Finally, Peter broke the silence.

"Does anyone want to say anything else? Any words of guidance or encouragement? Anything to help give her peace of mind?"

"This was very brave," said Zara. "Being angry is not healthy. We can't dwell on what happened because it will create a storm in us. Your father is with God, and you have your mother, so give thanks that you are safe. May God grant you peace and success in your studies and for the rest of your life."

"*Nagode*," said Falmata, holding Zara's gaze.

"*Nagode*."

"This was very brave," Laraba said reassuringly. "She is compassionate and brave. Despite all the adversity she faced, she continues to live. She's brought herself here to us, and to encourage others to keep living. She is reinventing herself. *Nagode*, Falmata."

"*Nagode*, Falmata. *Nagode*. *Nagode*." The girls in the circle all voiced quiet thanks. When they were done, Peter looked around.

"Gambo, are you ready to share with us?"

Gambo fidgeted in her seat, tugged at her black mesh veil, and took a deep breath. She wasn't sure she was ready to tell a group of strangers about the worst experience of her life. She hadn't talked about her time in the forest to anyone, not even her mother. She and Zara and Asma'u had exchanged anecdotes, but despite their growing friendship over the past few years, they had never truly shared their stories. She tugged at her veil again and looked around the circle. Laraba gave her a gentle smile and a slight nod, as if to say, "It's okay—this is a safe space." Zara and Asma'u also gave her encouraging smiles, so she took a deep breath and decided she would tell an abbreviated version of her story.

"It was on a Friday in 2014. Boko Haram came into our town shooting at everyone. We tried to escape but could not. They gathered us in the centre of our town, where men with guns watched us. If you tried to follow the mountain path, you [would] be killed. If you tried to escape another way, you [would] be killed. So we all lived with them in the city. They said, 'We have summoned you, and you must know that you are going to be married. And if you don't give in to us, we will kill your father, or we will give him a bomb and make him go and blow himself up.'

"So our parents said, 'It is better they marry you.' We prayed to God, even though we knew that He would not be able to get us out of this situation anytime soon. So we lived with them, and we accepted their laws.

"They were cruel. They would look for someone who had wronged them and accuse him of a crime, then they got the people together to judge the person. Those who did not convert to Islam were killed. We lived in our village with them like this for some time.

"They then said, 'We will take you to our forest,' and they loaded us into cars and drove to the Sambisa. We lived there with them. They took us all as brides, and we were all married. The unmarried women were left alone to stay with their mothers, but when the day came for you to get married, you got married. You didn't have a choice."

Gambo paused for a second and looked around. Little Aisha was fidgeting on Zara's lap. Asma'u was looking at the ground. Falmata was picking at a nail on her hand. They all knew what it was like to have no choice in the forest. Gambo took a breath and continued.

"Another woman told us, 'I know I'm not going out, but my advice to the rest of you is that when the planes come, you should hide. Be careful when the planes come because Boko Haram soldiers will try to shoot them down. They may even try to kill the pilots. To them, this is a war and they are ready to fight; their minds are not on the forest. If you see or hear any signs of planes, you must find a way to escape from them.' We told her we would follow her advice.

"Finally, the planes arrived. The Boko Haram soldiers decided to use fire. They set fire to the forest in their efforts to take down the planes. So we saw a chance to escape with my mother, my younger sister, my four siblings. We left the camp. We ran and ran. We later met other women along the way. We ran for four days, just wanting to put distance between ourselves and them. They probably thought we would return after the bombings and the fighting, and they would go from house to house and search. If anyone had given us refuge, they would be killed. They asked neighbours to tell on each other; it was an endless cycle of fear.

"We knew they were following us, asking anyone along the path if they had seen us. So we had to keep moving. We would rest for short periods and [eat] fruit from trees. It did not rain during those four days. Then we saw soldiers coming, and they approached us. We told them we had escaped the forest. The soldiers asked us if we had family members still in the forest. I told them no, we did not leave anyone behind in the forest. The rest of our family is in Gulak, outside of Madagali. The soldiers gave us food and water, and they offered to take us back home to Gulak. So they took us home, to our house in Gulak where our grandfather lived. He was relieved to have us back but worried. He told us to stay in the house.

"But life outside of the forest has not been easy. It's a different form of torture. You are constantly abused and mocked [because] you escaped Boko Haram. It's not different from being held captive by Boko Haram. You are considered as part of them. Since you lived with Boko Haram, you are capable of the things they are; you can also kill someone if you feel they have wronged you. So we are not good enough to mix with our own community. We are not good enough to work, not even on a farm. We are struggling. There is no food, no matter where we live. And as for schooling? There is no money for us to go back to school."

Gambo sighed. Hassana, the smallest girl in the room, fidgeted uncomfortably. She stole a glance at Gambo, but then quickly turned her attention back to her feet. Gambo didn't notice and carried on with her story.

"A foreigner came to help my mother for a little while. She was able to send two of my brothers to school, and she gave my mother some money to buy food and beans to make her cakes. If my mom was working, she would make five pounds of bean cakes. But now, she cannot even sell half a pound.

"We are struggling to come to terms with what we have done wrong. And so we live, sit, and work day by day and we hope to make some progress. We have to buy food, simple things like soap and pencils, things my siblings need for school.

"Also, we are treated like pariahs in our town. People gossip about us, [saying] that we are of Boko Haram. We are suffering so much even in our home village of Gulak. I'm not in school anymore. But I'm going to Islamic school, which is free, because my mother does not have the money to send me to school. Food is important, but it is God's will. No one buys our goods, our bean cakes, the little things we put out to sell. We are struggling and our father is dead, and there is no one to help us. I stay at home with my mother. I am happy that my two younger siblings are at school, but I wish I could go as well. We don't have much to eat, so food is more important than school for me."

Gambo stopped. She decided to end her story there. She looked down at her hands.

Peter nodded. "Thank you for sharing, Gambo." He looked around the room. "Falmata?"

Falmata looked at Gambo, who kept looking down. "*Nagode*. We have all experienced the same thing. One thing I can tell you is what we are learning here is that we have to accept this has happened and move on. If you keep thinking about it too much, you will not be able to study or focus on anything else."

Gambo mumbled, "*Nagode*." The other girls then thanked Gambo for her story. Zara told her she was brave for living through what she had. Laraba told her she was brave for sharing her experience with the group. Then she asked Maryam if she would like to speak.

Maryam, who was seated to the right of Asma'u, propped her left elbow up on the back of Asma'u's chair. She smiled slightly, as if to make herself more comfortable with the story she was about to tell. She would keep it short, but she started the same way the others did: with the day Boko Haram arrived in her village, as if that was a demarcation line between lives— life before and life after the devastation.

With each account, the girls started to open up, offer condolences and advice. The initial hesitation melted away, replaced by a spirit of community inspired by a shared experience. They were not alone; they had never been alone.

When it came time for Asma'u to have the floor, she surprised herself by how much she wanted to speak, to tell her story. It had come out in little bits before, but now she felt she could be fully heard.

"Boko Haram came to our town on a Saturday. When they arrived, we were working on the farm with my mother, me and my younger brothers and sisters. We ran when we knew they were coming—we tried to climb over the big rock to the other side. When we arrived, the Christians there said they wouldn't let us pass because we were Muslims. They said we should go back to our Boko Haram brothers. We should go back because Boko Haram are Muslims. We said no. They said we should go back or they [would] kill us themselves! But we could not go back, so we went through another city and were told it was also closed to us. We tried to turn around, but we ended up meeting [Boko Haram] on the road and so we quickly ran into a church. They asked us, 'Where are you going?' They said, 'You have to go back with us, back to your town. Why do you want to run away from us? Wherever you go, we'll go too. And if you don't come with us, our men will come back or kill you.' So they took us back into town. We were prisoners in our own home. They took our father with them and went to the forest. And to this day, we don't know where they took him. We have never seen him since that day."

Asma'u paused, playing with the fabric of her blue-and-white wrapper, folding a crease over and over.

"After many days of sitting at home, the news came: the soldiers are coming, and they're going to take back the city. So the Boko Haram men took us to the forest. They gathered us together and they went to war. Whoever married them was allowed to eat; they were using food to force us to marry them. We had to be good companions. We were not allowed to leave.

"Finally, one day they told my mother that they were going to take me. My mother and I both cried. They said they were going to take me and she said no, she won't let me go. They threatened to kill me if she refused to let me go. Then my mother said she preferred to be killed than to have me taken away. She didn't have a choice. I didn't have a choice. They said I belonged to Shekau.

"My religion was gone. I lived in a place with them, but I don't even know where I was. We had to go to their the Islamic classes, and they even gave us arms and knives. They said it was not going so well, and so they had to recruit more people to fight. One day, an aircraft came and started to bomb the place—everything was on fire. We then decided that when the plane comes, we could find a way to escape. Then we agreed on this. We fled and ran, and that is when we met other women and they asked me, 'Aren't you Hauwa's daughter?' I was shocked. I said, 'Yes! I am!' And they told me, 'Your mother was there. We left her in the forest. She said she would escape.' I thought I wouldn't see her, but then she came and found me, right there, in the middle of us fleeing the forest—she found me, so we fled together.

"We came across some vigilantes, hunters. They stopped us and took us to the army. Then they took us to their place and told the army soldiers, 'These are the ones we found on the road.'

The soldiers gave us food and asked if we had family nearby. We said yes, we had, but we didn't know where they were. We told them we were from Mubi. They said that since Boko Haram was still in control of our town, we should not go there because of attacks. So we went to Gulak, where we found our grandfather.

"We lived there for a while and started a small business selling bean cakes, but people would not buy anything from us. And they accused us of being threats to the community, of bringing death to them because we came out of Boko Haram's hands. And because we did, we almost certainly had their nature, and we did what they did. But then my mother found someone who helped us. Someone who gave us some money so we were able to buy food and feed the smaller children. My brother has been able to go back to school. But my younger sister and I are still not back."

She stopped. There was no more to say. Her life ended here, in limbo. Peter thanked her and then asked if anyone had any advice for her.

Maryam spoke up. "I would advise that you leave everything to God. Pray. Be thankful you are well, safe, and alive. And leave everything else to God. Keep your head held high, no matter what happens. Everything will get better."

Asma'u nodded without looking at Maryam and murmured, "*Nagode*."

No one else volunteered to speak right away. It was as if the weight of each word, each girl's story, needed time to settle before anyone could move on.

Aisha had been set down, and the little girl wandered between chairs before stopping in front of Gambo, who bent over and stroked the top of her head, welcoming the distraction. The horrors being shared—of lives torn apart, parents killed and missing—seemed more real somehow when spoken aloud.

Zara was next. She had been ready to share from the moment she thought about trying to find a "mind doctor." She gave a more detailed account of her story, beginning as the others had with the day Boko Haram came to her village, and ending with the news that she was excited to be enrolled in a boarding school to continue her education.

Peter and Laraba thanked her, then asked the room whether anyone had advice for her. To her own surprise, Asma'u spoke up.

"I would tell you to be patient," she said softly, trying to find the right words. "It is terrible we have all suffered from these experiences, but God knows best for us. He has brought us out of the forest, and He will guide us to what is next."

"Thank you, Asma'u," Peter said.

He stopped for a moment to let Zara's story sit with the group. Little Aisha was now on Laraba's lap, having procured a second lollipop from the counsellor's purse. Peter looked around the room. There was only one more story left to hear. He looked at the smallest girl of the group, the one sitting next to Dr. Akilu.

"Hassana," he said softly, "are you ready to speak?" The girl took a sharp inhale and gave an imperceptible nod.

"Please, everyone," he said. "Listen to her story."

15
HASSANA'S STORY

HASSANA SA'IDU HAD been silent all this time, listening and dabbing at her eyes as the stories poured out from the other girls. She sat in her chair in the circle, her feet dangling, barely touching the floor. Now she shuffled her legs back and forth, her shoes scraping the floor, making a small noise that broke the silence as everyone waited for her to speak.

Her eyes, dark with defiance, darted around the room, gauging how safe this space was and what she could say. She then rested her gaze on Laraba, who nodded at her. When she spoke, everyone looked up. Her voice belied her small stature; she spoke in a low staccato, her words piercing the air.

"On Friday mornings, my routine was usually to prepare the meals for the day and tidy the house. I was going with a friend of my parents' to her sister's wedding that day. I remember she brought her dress into the house and was getting ready, and she invited me to go with her. So we went together to the mosque for the ceremony. I remember it started to rain when we got there; it started to rain very, very hard. That was when we heard gunshots. And then it happened so fast. One of the wedding guests was hit. And then men with guns ran into the town, announcing that they were Boko Haram.

"Whenever they fired a gun, they would shout, 'Allahu Akbar!' And then they would reload that weapon. Soldiers and Boko Haram were fighting in the town. The men started gathering the townspeople together. They forced our teachers and pregnant and married women to be gathered in one place; men were being assembled separately. They said, 'You either kill someone or you will be killed.' In every three, there [was] one who refused. And they went out and killed the men. After they had killed the men, they would come and marry their wives. The teachers are in heaven now, as are the men who were killed with them."

Hassana's voice broke. That last line was something that had come to her in recent months, a thought that gave her some relief. She repeated it.

"The teachers are in heaven now.

"After they sat us down, they fired a shot. They kicked the door open. They came in and asked, 'Where are the teachers?' We said we did not have teachers. 'You have killed them. They are gone.'

"So they said, 'Come with us; we are taking you away.' They told the women, 'Your daughters are going to have children for us.' Then they took us and left. We spent three days in the forest. We did not have food to eat. We spent three days just as we were—we weren't allowed to bring anything with us.

"There was a woman there. I called her Aunty—she had four children, and I was helping her. I did not know where my parents were."

Hassana seemed to lose track of her story. She talked about being taken into the forest by Boko Haram, but then she and the aunty were suddenly leaving the forest and trying to find their way home. And then she told the group that she was back in Gwoza, her village, where Boko Haram had assumed control. She was speaking faster. No one seemed to notice. The other girls gave her their full attention; their own stories were so similar. All of them living their trauma through Hassana's.

"They gathered us together in a school. It was a big school. And they did the same thing as before, separating the women and the men. They took the men away. We said we were thirsty, and they brought us this dirty water. We didn't want to drink it because it was dirty, but we had no choice. After I drank it, I felt like I was out of my body. They asked me where my mother was, and I said I did not have a mother there. I don't know where my mother is. They brought the aunty to me and said, 'Here, this is your mother.' Another girl was there with both her father and her mother, and they cut her father's throat right in front of her. The girl was crying. We were all crying. They told us to be quiet."

Hassana's voice dropped off here. She looked down at her hands and squeezed her eyes shut. The room was silent, save for a muffled sob. She opened her eyes and let out an audible shudder. "Then they gave me a knife. They told me I had to cut the aunty who was my mother. I was out of my body, my mind. I cut her. I cut her."

She buried her face in the folds of her headscarf and sobbed. The others looked at her blankly. This was not the turn they'd expected her story to take. Hassana had taken a different path, one they knew about but never thought possible. Gambo's big eyes widened. She had imagined herself taking revenge on her captors and slicing their throats, one by one, with a big gleaming knife. But she never thought she would be forced to kill someone innocent, someone like her aunt or her mother. She wasn't sure she could hold a knife to even the cruellest of the Boko Haram wives, let alone her own mother, her aunty. She looked at the sobbing girl with a new regard.

Hassana's chest heaved with the weight of her tears. Her right hand made a fist, as if she was ready to punish herself. She buried her head in her hands. The two counsellors and Dr. Akilu let the silence hang, giving her the space she needed to do whatever she felt she had to.

After a few minutes, she raised her head. Tears were still streaming down her cheeks. She continued.

"She was lying down and I cut her. I killed her. I looked down at her and I made peace with her. I still dream about this sometimes. And the headaches still haunt me. I deserve this. I do not mind having to live with the headaches. It is my conscience crying out to me.

"Then they ordered me to bury the woman. So I dragged her body and buried her myself. That day, I buried myself. It was a different body, but it may as well have been me."

The room was silent again as she hid her face in her scarf. Her body convulsed, as if rejecting the memory.

Zara's eyes were closed. Asma'u fidgeted with her phone, twirling it between her fingers, first on her right hand, then her left. She thought about how they had tried to teach her to shoot a gun, use a knife. Hassana seemed to need to gather her strength in between memories. When she started again, her staccato had slowed, her voice now heavy with resignation.

"I should have left then, just left. But they won't let you go. I don't even know what I was worth. I did what they asked of me. I did it because my mind was not in my body. We had to get out of there. They taught us how to shoot with a gun. They taught us how to make bombs, to kill anyone and cut anything.

"They brought someone else to see us—someone who showed us a metal thing in a jar that was broken. He was making a bomb, he explained. He would set it off, and then go and hide somewhere. They put the bomb in the road, but I never heard it go off. And then the man who made the bomb was stabbed by the others. He was killed. We were all crying. It was madness. No one cared about us. Everybody was on their own.

"One night, there were more bombs and everything was red. There was blood everywhere. We decided to run because everything was red and no one was watching us. We walked for most of that first day and for nine days after that. The days were long, and there was no water and hunger tormented us. The wind, the hunger. We were so hungry, but there was no food anywhere. If we saw water, we drank even if it was bad water.

"After many days, we finally arrived in Madagali. We were taken to the police station, where we were greeted by an aunty and not by family members. We were told to sit down, and they started to ask us a lot of questions. We were there, at the station, for three days. We ended up staying for three months at the house of the aunty. But she was worried about me because my mind was not well. I would wake up crying about everything and nothing. I could not focus on anything. I wanted to study, and the aunty told me I would study, so we decided I would come to Maiduguri. They found my mother, and she came to be with me.

"When I first got here, I was not well. I sat in my room and just felt the tears come down. It was very hot. I had no peace of mind. My mind was gone. They took me to the hospital and gave me medicines. But I couldn't sleep. I would lie on the floor; I didn't want the bed. Women came to clean me, give me fresh clothes. They gave me more medicines to help me sleep, but I think it was too strong because then I started to see things in my head. My hands would be shaking, the same hand that held the knife. My mother could not help me. I saw snakes everywhere. 'Mother, snakes!' I would scream, and I would try to run, but there was nowhere to go. They're demons. The snakes were demons. They were problems, and they slithered into my body and into my mind. They gave me more medicine, but I came to understand that the medicine they gave me was much too powerful. It feels like my hands are bound and I have night terrors, hallucinations that haunt me in my sleep."

Zara would later say she was relieved to hear Hassana speak about her nightmares because it was something Zara had not been able to talk to anyone about. It made her feel a little better to know that other girls had brought the same dreams back from the forest.

Hassana continued her stream of consciousness.

"'Oh, I want to sleep forever,' I was praying to God. 'Please hear my prayers.' Sometimes in my sleep, my father comes back. I don't know where he came from, but he is there and I am accused by a crowd that I killed my father!

"Whenever I have this dream, I would say to my mother, to the aunty, 'Boko Haram are back! Aunty, Boko Haram are going to kill me!'

"Sometimes I see the woman. The one I cut. She comes to me at night. But it all seems like threats by the demon. Sometimes I feel like the demon, the snake, is in my body. They say they will kill me. I have had the same dream for some weeks now. My mother and I are talking like everything is normal, and then suddenly there is a bomb. A bomb that is dropped into our home. And it blew up everyone. It just blew up everyone.

"But you know something? I am not afraid anymore. I suffered in their hands and I survived them. This pain in my heart is like a gun that I carry. If you bring me a gun, I will shoot. I can shoot a man. I killed a woman. Right now, there is no fear in my heart, even for a minute. But I am suffering in my own way. I am safe. But there will always be a pain. May God protect and heal us all."

Hassana had run out of words. Her cheeks were streaked with dried tears, and she looked around the room defiantly. Her story was on the table. Her pain laid bare. She wasn't sure what she was hoping for in terms of a reaction, but the stunned and silent faces staring blankly into space told her all she needed to know. She was alone in this room in a way. None of the other girls had stepped over the line between captive and collaborator. None of them had to kill—not just another human being but a part of themselves—just to survive. No one else would understand the depth of the torment she was now burdened with.

The others stared into space, unmoving. What Hassana had revealed was beyond anything they had experienced themselves; the nightmare of their own time in the forest seemed less horrific in the face of this small girl's extraordinary confession. She had been forced to kill. Did that make her experience worse? Would they have done the same? There were so many questions.

The counsellors knew that Hassana had shifted the atmosphere in the room. Laraba spoke first. "We are all going to breathe. In and out. Put your hands on your knees and breathe in."

The girls took a collective breath in and let an audible breath out.

"Keep breathing, try to relax."

Peter's voice was softer than earlier. "In and out, in and out."

After a few moments, Dr. Akilu spoke, and she said what they had all been thinking. "The truth is that all your experiences—everything that happened to each of you—are similar. But those of you who have worked with Peter and Aunty Laraba, maybe you can tell the others how that has helped."

Hassana spoke first. "Yes, it has helped a lot," she said.

Zara looked at her quizzically and asked, "How did it help? Because you are still crying when you speak about it. You are still crying."

Dr. Akilu smiled at Zara, and then she put an arm around Falmata and spoke softly to her. "Do you remember when you first came here? You couldn't speak about what had happened for a very long time, and it was hard to start to talk about it."

Falmata nodded.

"But then you could sit with Aunty Laraba and talk to her," Dr. Akilu continued, "and she comforted you and let you speak. And you can speak without fear that you will lose your mind,

because Laraba validates everything you tell her. It's your experience, but that's what we are here for—to help you come to
terms with it, and to help you move on. That's why we brought
these girls here—they have never had the experience of being
able to speak to someone like Laraba or Peter."

Falmata nodded again, and then she spoke in a louder voice
than the one she'd used earlier to tell her story. "At first I used to
think about it a lot, but now that I'm starting to study and talk
about it, it is easier. I had intended to try to forget about everything that happened. But sometimes, the thoughts return to me,
so I distract myself by reading my book—I love to read—and
when I'm reading, I am in another place. I'm able to let it go.
And I say to myself, 'I can do this!'

"The other students have been a great help to me. This year,
I was the top student in my class. And I know I'm not alone. I
want to encourage other students, too, to look forward to the
future. And not to think that life is over, because I refuse to
believe that. I believe that I can make my future better. And
God willing, whatever you want, if you believe you can do it,
you will do it."

Falmata smiled, looking at Asma'u, Gambo, and Zara in turn.

"Does anyone have anything they would like to ask her?"
Laraba's voice broke the short silence.

At this point, Gambo got up and left the room. She walked
down the hall, found a door leading to an alcove, and stood alone
for a while, her back to the window. She needed to find a way
to breathe again before she could come back; she had suddenly
realized that she was broken into many pieces and she didn't
know how to put herself back together.

The others let her go. Inside, Zara spoke, making amends for her friend who left.

She caught Falmata's eye and smiled. "I just want to thank you for speaking with us, and for allowing us to come here. This helps us a lot, to know that we are not alone. We pray that God helps you with His grace, that you continue your studies. And that we also are able to continue our studies."

Aisha ran from person to person until Laraba picked her up and put the little girl on her lap.

"*Inshallah!*" Falmata smiled back at Zara.

Dr. Akilu spoke as the girls broke up into smaller groups. "One of you will go with Peter and the other with Aunty Laraba. Because this has been such an intensive session, we'll need to spend some time alone with each of you, to make sure we can keep moving forward."

The girls were now talking among themselves like teenage girls the world over. Falmata was looking at something on Zara's phone. Asma'u and Maryam spoke softly before dissolving into giggles. Then the girls separated into their groups, following the two counsellors out of the conference room.

"Their stories are horrific," Fatima said after the intense group therapy session. "They have all been through a trauma, but there are degrees." She explained that Hassana had to leave Lafiya Sariri for a while in the beginning. She just could not cope with her experience and brought it to every aspect of her life. After working with her in a different setting, they eventually brought her back to the school. "I'm very proud of her," the doctor said, "and the work she has put in to get to where she is now."

There was another girl, Fatima recalled, who had a baby with her Boko Haram husband and was rescued along with the child after the father was killed by government forces. Fatima saw the girl stomping on her baby, willing him to die, because he was "born of the devil." She understood that the kind of trauma these girls were facing is intergenerational, but she believed it was possible to end the cycle. She tried not to think of the girls her organization couldn't reach—the thousands like Gambo, Zara, and Asma'u who were forced to go back to their villages without resources, without support. Many had returned to the forest, to Boko Haram, where they did not have to suffer the shame that marked every survivor of the group. In the Sambisa, they were all bound by the same fate; there was no one to judge them.

The volleyball game was in full swing in the yard of the school. Girls dove for the ball, cheered each other on when a point was scored, giggled when they fumbled. Hassana stood against the school building with three other girls, watching the action, her dark eyes following the white ball as it was lobbed from one side of the net to the other. When one of the players said she had to go inside, the facilitator looked around the yard for a substitute.

"Hassana," he said, "come on."

Hassana seemed unsure. Her eyes rested on the net with the ball no longer in motion. She hesitated. The girl standing next to her gave her a nudge. She was still uncertain.

"Come on!" The pleas came from several girls on the make-shift court. "Hassana! Hassana!"

She shifted her weight from one foot to the other.

"We need you!"

Her friend nudged her again, and finally Hassana straightened, smiled, and jogged into position.

16
OPTIONS

A WEEK AFTER the visit to Maiduguri and Lafiya Sariri, Gambo returned to her cousin Ibrahim's house in Yola. She was washing herself in the morning, performing careful ablutions for prayer. Since leaving the forest, she had become even more devout and now prayed five times a day. The Islamic teachings forced on them while they were captive had worked their way into her consciousness. It was not only a way to mark and pass time in the forest but also a part of the day that she and the other girls had looked forward to because they were able to gather. Now, alone, she carefully washed her face, her arms, her hands, and her feet, laying out her wrapper on the dusty earth outside her cousin's home. She bowed her head several times, touching her forehead to the ground, reciting the prayers for the morning *fajr*. She was going to Islamic school at the mosque in her village. It was free, and it was a small consolation for the fact that her mother couldn't afford to send her to the public school a village away.

She had also met a man. His name was Muhammad, and they met when he stopped to buy Hajera's *akara*. He started talking to Hajera first, keeping his eyes on Gambo the entire time. As they spent more time together, away from the *akara* stand, she came to see he was quite a decent person. She liked the way his eyes danced when he spoke to her. Most of all, he did not seem to care that she had once spent time in the Sambisa. He also had not finished school—he sold SIM cards for mobile phones at a local corner stand. His family had no more than hers; their only real difference was that she had spent time in the forest and he had not. They didn't speak much about it, but he knew that she had been married while she was held captive, and that she had eventually managed to escape. He wasn't interested in anything else and didn't ask her any embarrassing questions about her time there. For that alone, she was grateful.

After a while, he proposed to her. It was not something she had ever thought of since she escaped the forest, if she was honest with herself. Before Boko Haram, she had always assumed she would marry eventually. But as a former Boko Haram wife, she understood her options were much more limited. Muhammad's offer was one she had to consider seriously, something her mother kept reminding her of.

For all of Gambo's praying, though, she could not rid herself of the anger that was roiling inside of her. It sometimes consumed her when she thought of all the wrongs that had been done to her in the Sambisa. It ate at her from the inside out, and she would seethe silently. She would force herself to shut her mind off from the memories to control the rage she felt. But that was difficult because all things led back to the forest. The time she was held captive was almost like a rebirth into a new life. A harder life. A life where nothing made sense and nothing was fair.

She was heading home from the Islamic school one afternoon when she saw a group of hunters coming back into the village. They were marching several men to the military station nearby. She later found out that the hunters were vigilantes who'd been deputized by the government to help rid the area of Boko Haram and rescue its prisoners. This intrigued her. She grew curious about how someone might join a hunter's group.

She never brought the subject up with her mother—she was certain Hajera would not take it seriously—but she mentioned it in her Islamic studies classes to some of her classmates. How could she find out more about what they did? Someone mentioned that there was a famous woman who led a hunting group out of Yola. Her name was Aisha, and she was as fierce as any Boko Haram commander. In fact, legend had it that she had killed more terrorists than any military chief.

At first, Gambo found it hard to believe that a woman could be capable of such violence. But the more she thought about it, the more she realized that perhaps *she* could also be capable. After all, hadn't she thought about killing her forest husband? Many times. Many, many times. Back then, she didn't think she could do it because she was sure she would be caught and punished. And punishment in the forest meant death. But as a vigilante, she could hunt and kill her captors and be on the right side of the law. Gambo decided she had to go to Yola to meet this woman who hunted Boko Haram.

In truth, the trip and the meeting were a distraction. Gambo was lacking direction. Now almost nineteen years old and unable to finish school, she was tired of selling *akara* alongside her mother. She wasn't sure she wanted to marry, but Hajera wanted her to accept Muhammad's proposal. It would be one less mouth to feed, and Gambo was getting older. If she didn't take a husband before she turned twenty, it would be almost impossible to find anyone who would want her. With no education and no husband, she was almost condemned to fry *akara* for the rest of her life. Neither Gambo nor her mother wanted that. But the offer of marriage was there, and it sounded better than standing in front of a vat of oil and bubbling bean cakes for eternity. Still, Aisha the Hunter might give her something else, a better alternative than the meagre choices before her.

After her morning *fajr*, Gambo carefully wrapped her hair in a brown-and-white *gele*, the same material as her wrapper. She draped a cream shawl over her shoulders and then applied kohl under her eyes and a shiny taupe shadow on her eyelids. She put on a pair of dangly earrings. She wanted to make a good impression. Her cousin Ibrahim accompanied her to Aisha's compound and let her out at the gate. Armed guards gave Gambo the once-over and ushered her into the courtyard, where Jamila and Chinara, two of Aisha's newest female recruits, were sitting.

Dressed in dark T-shirts and fatigue-style pants, the two couldn't have been a starker contrast to Gambo, who looked like a beauty queen. They eyed her curiously, wondering what would bring such a creature to their compound.

The Queen Hunter, Aisha, came out of her room, Sa'adatu on her hip. "*Sannu! Sannu!*" Her smile widened as the child tried to wriggle out of her hold. She motioned to her husband, Muhammadu, to take the child. Sa'adatu refused to go with her father. Muhammadu laughed and sat down at the edge of the courtyard, ready to take her if needed. A few other hunters who had been milling around the courtyard joined him. Aisha looked at Gambo. "Please come inside." She gestured to an opening to the sitting room, which was next to the bedroom. All the rooms were in a row. There were no doors, so they all looked out onto the courtyard, where Jamila and Chinara were sitting.

"What's your name again?" Aisha asked.

"Gambo."

"Gambo, that's right. Where are you from?"

"Gulak."

"Ah, Gulak. We were there a while ago, when they thought Boko Haram was about to launch another attack. Do you remember? I think that was . . . last year?"

Gambo nodded. She remembered seeing the hunters on patrol, but she didn't remember seeing Aisha among them, much less leading them.

Aisha sensed Gambo's hesitation. "Let's take it easy. Were you abducted and taken away?"

"Yes." Gambo's voice was low. "They took us into the forest."

The women talked softly. Aisha wanted to know how Gambo had escaped, and how many people she knew were left in the forest. She wanted to know how far into the Sambisa Gambo had been taken so she could try to map out where she might lead her group next, where they might find other captives and perhaps capture some more Boko Haram members. Gambo described it the best she could, speaking as if she were simply narrating another person's experience, keeping distance between herself and what had happened to her in the forest.

Aisha started talking about a successful operation they had recently completed near the Sambisa, north of where they were now. It was a mission she was pleased with—they had apprehended four Boko Haram fighters, one of whom was the son of a commander. And they were just preparing to go into Yobe State on a patrol. The government was worried that Boko Haram was expanding its reach westward. The group was already a menace in neighbouring countries like Cameroon and Chad, but the authorities were less concerned with its activities outside Nigeria's borders. Until recently, the fighters had not made any attempts to terrorize communities outside of Borno and Adamawa States. Their incursion into Yobe had raised alarms, and the Civilian Joint Task Force had been charged with preventing the extremists from gaining too much territory.

And then it was Gambo's turn to ask questions. "Do you have military escorts with you to protect you?" she asked. She somehow couldn't imagine Aisha, this female hunter, leading a group into the forest on her own. She thought of the two girls she'd seen in the courtyard. One seemed too small and meek for such a calling.

"Sometimes we do, sometimes we don't. It depends if they are busy. It doesn't really matter to us." Aisha shrugged. Sometimes it was easier for them to go alone.

"But what if you run into Boko Haram?" Gambo was having

trouble wrapping her head around the concept of confronting militants without reinforcements.

"That mission when we apprehended four people?" Aisha said. "We were alone. No one challenged us."

Gambo shook her head, incredulous. "Those people will never repent. They have no concept of remorse."

"Maybe," Aisha said. "But the situation is better there now. The governor and the people have been really cooperative with us, and they are vigilant."

Gambo looked around. She gestured past the door to the courtyard at Jamila and Chinara. "Are they going to the forest with you?" she asked.

Aisha nodded. "They are ready. They have been training for a long time now."

"And what about him?" Gambo pointed at Muhammadu, who was not wearing attire suited for hunting.

"Which one? The tall one?" Aisha followed her finger. "That is my husband."

"Does he go to the forest with you?"

"No." Sa'adatu was clamouring over Aisha, reaching for Gambo.

"This is your child?" Gambo hadn't known that Aisha was married, let alone a mother.

"Yes, this is Sa'adatu. She wanted to sleep when you arrived, so she's confused. This is usually her nap time."

"Are you still feeding her?" This opened a whole new avenue of interest for Gambo. She had imagined this fierce woman hunter to be just that—a hunter. She hadn't even thought that Aisha would have a family.

"I'm weaning her. It won't be an issue when we go to Yobe this week. She's a year and a month now, so she should be weaning anyway."

"How long will you be in Yobe?"

"Maybe a week. We're not sure yet."

"Are you going to arrest Boko Haram there?" Gambo's eyes widened.

"If we come across them, we will apprehend them and bring them to the station."

Gambo tried to imagine a fighter surrendering, being captured. She had only known them the way a captive knows her torturer. She found it hard to picture them as the ones being led into custody, being held accountable for their crimes.

"Tell me something," Gambo asked. "When you take them into custody and they are still alive, do they often repent? Are they sorry for what they've done?"

"Most of them are unrepentant," Aisha said. "Some are sorry they have been arrested, but not truly sorry for their actions. There are programs the government and other organizations have set up to help them become repentant."

"Do you think they work?" Gambo had a hard time believing any Boko Haram soldier would be able to convert.

Aisha shrugged. After she handed over the men she arrested to the authorities, she rarely had the time to follow up. It was always onto the next mission. She did recall giving over a few dozen men to the authorities in Mubi, only to find out weeks later that all of them had gone back to the forest. She was so discouraged that she sat out a few patrols.

"What about the girls you rescue?" Gambo had so many questions. She wanted to know how other girls were adjusting, and whether Aisha kept in touch with any of the ones she brought out of the forest.

Aisha shook her head. Sometimes it was hard to think about.

"There were three girls we brought out, and we took them back to their village. They all ended up going back to the forest."

"What?" This was shocking to Gambo. "Why would anyone choose to go back?"

"They found that life in their village was too difficult. There was no food. No one to help them. Their own people shunned them. They decided it was better to go back."

Gambo was stunned. As difficult as it had been for her to find her footing in Gulak, she had never been tempted to go back to the forest. How much worse would it have to get for her to take such drastic action? Never.

"We saved one woman three times," Aisha continued. "She still went back. The last time, when the military was with us and she was with the Boko soldiers, they shot her."

"They shot her?"

"She was with the militants, and they starting shooting at us. The soldiers who were travelling with us shot back and hit her."

Gambo was speechless. Aisha spoke about killing Boko Haram with the same nonchalance that the extremists spoke about killing civilians. Suddenly, she wasn't sure if this was a path for her after all. But the thought of going back to selling bean cakes was even less appealing.

"Are you recruiting new members for your team?" she asked.

"Always," Aisha responded. "Our work is not done, and the government keeps asking us to go to new areas. This scourge will only spread further if it is not stopped."

And with that, Aisha excused herself to prepare for their trek to Yobe. She motioned for Muhammadu to take their daughter while she conferred with the other hunters. She smiled at Gambo. "Jamila and Chinara would be pleased to answer any more questions you might have," she said.

Gambo thanked her and slowly approached the two women, who were sitting not far from Muhammadu on a raised wooden platform that ran across the entrances to the four rooms that made up the house. It overlooked the dusty courtyard.

"Do you mind if I ask you some questions?" Gambo gathered the bottom of her wrapper and sat down.

The two women nodded, studying her more closely. They hid their skepticism behind an earnest attempt to answer her queries.

Gambo asked what the training involved and how long they'd been away. She wanted to know if they'd learned to fire a gun, and if they thought they would be able to use it effectively. Would they be able to hit their target in the confusion of a battle? This question was directed more at Chinara, who was smaller than most women Gambo had met. She could not imagine this tiny creature taking part in a battle against Boko Haram, let alone firing a rifle to kill one of their soldiers.

"We have trained hard for more than a year now, and we are ready when the time comes." Chinara's voice was childlike, the complete opposite of Gambo's own drawn-out guttural syllables.

"Why did you decide to join?"

"We wanted to be able to help ourselves and other girls, and get rid of this problem in our country."

It was clear from the way she was speaking that Jamila saw this as obvious, but it wasn't at all obvious to Gambo. She was considering it because she needed an outlet for her anger, and she didn't like her other options. She also wanted revenge, something that was not sanctioned in the Qur'an. She carried this truth shamefully in her heart. It might be a good reason to join the hunters, but she wondered whether she would be able to kill when the time came. She lingered a little longer, asking the same questions again, asking herself at the same time.

Jamila and Chinara were patient, answering every question honestly and thoughtfully. Jamila, Gambo learned, was a distant cousin of Aisha's, so it was easy for her to fall in with the group. Chinara was inspired by stories of the hunters rescuing women who had been captured by Boko Haram.

"We have to do our part," she said earnestly. "This problem affects us all, and we, as women, must stand up for ourselves and protect each other."

Later, Gambo's cousin Ibrahim asked her about the meeting.

"You're not really thinking of joining the vigilantes, are you?"

Gambo had trouble finding an answer. "I don't know," she said. "I don't know."

It was as if the life that had been set out for her before Boko Haram was gone forever. She was now drifting aimlessly, unsure which direction she should point herself in. If she had only been able to finish school, she might have been on the path to a real job by now, or even university. Everything seemed harder—impossible, even. She shuffled her feet on the dusty floor and bit her lip.

"I really don't know."

Gambo looked down at this little creature, so small. She could not believe she was real. "*Sannu,*" she whispered to the child. The baby was making a gurgling noise, and it looked like she was smiling. Gambo gently stroked her head and ran her index finger over her impossibly tiny hands. She felt as if all her fears about her future had been erased by this one little being.

After her trip to meet Aisha Gombi and her hunting group, Gambo returned to Gulak, mulling her choices. She was selling her mother's *akara* to help pass the time, but she knew she would have to make some decisions about what she wanted to do. That was when she discovered she was pregnant. It had come as a surprise to her and everyone around her, including the baby's father, Muhammad. At first, she wasn't sure she wanted to keep the baby. She had never planned on being a mother. But then Muhammad stepped in and repeated his offer of marriage; he would bring her and the child who was on the way into his home as his family. She wouldn't have to work or sell bean cakes anymore. Gambo still wasn't certain, but Hajera saw this as her best option. Here was a man who was willing to overlook her Boko Haram past. Gambo was getting too old to remain at home, and her chances for marriage would diminish as she got older. Hajera saw this as a gift for her family, to marry off her eldest daughter to a decent man. She was worried when Gambo had talked about meeting Aisha. She didn't want to hear any more nonsense about joining the vigilantes.

And so, Gambo's decision was made for her. She and Muhammad married, and she moved into his home with his parents. It was not as difficult an adjustment as she feared. Muhammad was almost completely obsessed with his new wife. And he had been thrilled when, on a Saturday morning in the fall of 2019, Gambo gave birth to a healthy baby girl.

She was content for now to be a mother, delighting in the baby's every giggle, every smile. She missed her siblings, but the baby filled every void in her life. And when her tiny hands reached up to Gambo, asking to be picked up, Gambo felt like her heart would burst. The baby was a fierce little creature, crying loudly when she was hungry and pushing her mother away when she was finished feeding.

Gambo decided to name her Aisha.

EPILOGUE

ZARA DECIDED TO change schools. She wanted to be closer to her daughter and her family and Bashir. The strain of being away for months at a time was wearing on her. It was also affecting her grades. Still, it was hard to leave her friends in Askira Uba, especially Amina, who had become almost like a sister to her.

Zara credited the counselling she received at Lafiya Sariri with finally allowing her to open up about her past. Peter and Laraba had convinced her that nothing that happened to her in the forest—and nothing that was still happening to her—was her fault. The shame and stigma of being a Boko Haram wife was not her problem. If the people in her town were so blinded by the violence that they couldn't see an innocent victim for who she was, that was their problem. She was finally beginning to understand that none of it was her fault, no matter what anyone else thought. She would no longer allow herself to be judged by people who were trivial to her life.

And so, after many months of hiding her other life from her best friend, she finally told Amina the truth. Amina had overheard her on a video call with her daughter and asked her who the baby was. Zara was tired of lying to her. She broke down and told Amina the story of how Boko Haram had attacked her village and taken her into the forest, of how she'd escaped, unknowingly carrying the baby back with her. Amina listened. And then she cried. She cried for everything her friend had endured and now had to bear. She cried for all the girls in her own village who had been taken when Boko Haram came. It turned out that Amina herself had escaped capture, but like most people in northeastern Nigeria, she had not been left untouched.

Zara cried with her, a rare moment when her true emotions broke through her thin veneer of strength. Amina hugged her friend, then looked into Zara's eyes. Tears ran down both cheeks, mingling in their clasped hands.

"You are so brave," she whispered. More tears poured out with those words.

Zara had never spoken about her trauma to anyone so bluntly and honestly. She had never felt comfortable enough to do it. The experience was too personal and too painful, and the stigma attached to it only exacerbated her discomfort and added to the weight of the truth she kept to herself. But somehow, this confession to Amina felt a bit like the beginning of an unburdening. Someone else now knew about her dark secret. Someone else now truly saw her.

It made leaving Askira Uba that much more difficult. But the girls promised to stay in touch and visit whenever they could.

Zara enrolled in a private boarding school in Yola. She still lived in a dormitory, but it was closer to her family and she could see them on weekends. But she continued to struggle in class.

Gone was the confidence she'd once had in school; that felt like a lifetime ago. She used to be the first to raise her hand to answer a question, to challenge a teacher about the way a verse was interpreted or correct a fellow student for a misspelling—gently, of course. But that was gone. Now she second-guessed her own instincts constantly, and the lessons were getting harder. It felt as if she had a mental block in math and science. Those two subjects were dragging her average down, and her self-esteem as well.

After two semesters, it became clear that Zara could not keep up with her classmates. The head teacher said she would need to leave, unless she wanted to repeat the year. Zara left and enrolled in a public school in her village. Despite encouragement from Bashir and her family, her enthusiasm for finishing her education was dwindling by the semester. But she told herself she had to at least get her high school diploma so she could find a decent job to support herself and Aisha. She tried not to dwell on the time lost and the path her life had taken. She revelled in her daughter, celebrating Aisha's every milestone and silently promising her that she would send her to the best schools possible when it was time. Aisha could be the college student Zara once dreamed she herself would be. Aisha could be the doctor her mother would never become. As she buried her own dreams, she planted them in her daughter. Aisha's future held the promises that were once Zara's. Promises that now seemed irreparably broken.

Asma'u also returned to school, but she performed even worse academically than Zara. She simply could not concentrate in

class. Her mind wandered, pondering everything in her universe except for the subject at hand. Her mother felt it was
a great inconvenience to have her out of the home. Hauwa
warned Asma'u that if she didn't pass at the end of the school
year, she wouldn't be allowed to repeat and would have to
come home to help with the housework and take care of her
younger siblings.

Asma'u did not pass her final exams and was doomed to
repeat her year, but she managed to transfer to a different school,
where, with the help of a tutor, she studied hard to advance to
the next level. Her mother allowed her this one last chance.

Like Zara, Asma'u did not remember school being this difficult, but she knew she had to press on. Living back at home with
Hauwa and her new husband was her least favourite option, so
she tried her best to focus on her schoolwork. If she could complete high school, she might be able to find a job and move out
of her mother's life.

Aisha Gombi continued to lead her group of hunters into the
forest. But as her daughter, Sa'adatu, got older, she started to pull
back. She trained her cousin Amina to gradually take on more
responsibilities and prepared the men to take orders from her.
There was also a waiting list of young women wanting to join
her in her mission, and she continued to mentor those who were
ready to dedicate themselves to the cause. The pull of motherhood was very strong, and she wanted to be home with her
daughter and husband. She wanted to be an active participant,
a full parent for Sa'adatu. But as long as Boko Haram continued

its violent rampage across the region, she knew she could never truly step aside.

In July 2019, Mama Boko Haram finally managed to convince Nneka's brother to release some girls into the care of her foundation. The commander himself did not surrender and lay down his arms. But it was a start, and better than nothing at all.

Later that year, Mama was arrested, along with her colleague Prince and another program manager from her charity, on charges of fraud. A trader alleged that the Complete Care and Aid Foundation had failed to pay him for 111 million naira (roughly US$310,000) worth of goods like maize and vehicles. He claimed that some of the contracts he had signed with her had been falsified.

Mama vehemently denied the accusations as politically motivated, a blatant attempt by the government to keep her from interfering with their war against Boko Haram. She and her co-defendants fought the charges against them from prison. Her health, according to David Otto, her UK-based advisor, deteriorated rapidly, and she had to be taken to the hospital on several occasions to be treated for high blood pressure and other issues.

On June 14, 2022, Mama and her co-defendants were convicted on charges of conspiracy and fraud. They were sentenced to five years in prison, with no option to pay a fine instead. Her family is concerned about her health and believes her life is at risk.

Gambo and her husband eventually separated. Her mother-in-law never liked the fact that her son was married to a former Boko Haram wife, and she finally forced Muhammad to divorce her. Gambo moved back into Hajera's house with her daughter, Aisha. She has never thought about going back to school.

Boko Haram continues to sow terror throughout the region and is still trying to expand its reach into the northwestern part of Nigeria. The government likes to boast that the group's members are surrendering in large numbers, but the reality is that the military still has little control over its activities in the Sambisa forest. Villages are overrun and girls taken on an almost weekly basis, and authorities are struggling to gain the upper hand in what has become a tug of war for territory—and captives.

The insurgency continues to cause insurmountable displacement issues. Millions of people throughout the Lake Chad area—Cameroon, Niger, and Chad—are living in IDP camps, victims of a terrible confluence of terrorism and, more recently, climate change. Years of drought have reduced farming and herding activities to nothing. Environmental scientists estimate that Lake Chad has lost 90 percent of its surface water in the last fifty years. And the parched land has contributed to the dwindling of other resources. Rather than competing for scarce jobs, many young men join militant groups like Boko Haram and its offshoot, ISWAP (Islamic State West Africa Province).

The captured girls who manage to escape—and there are still no estimates on the total number—must find a way within themselves to move forward with their lives without any help and somehow come to terms with the destruction that the violence has wrought. Their struggle to find themselves anew, and to navigate an uncertain and often unforgiving future, is a testament to the strength of their characters, their determination to overcome the evil that befell them, and their steadfast refusal to be held captive by their collective trauma.

Gambo, Asma'u, and Zara in Yola, 2019.

ACKNOWLEDGEMENTS

THIS BOOK WOULD not have been possible without the brave and beautiful young women who trusted me to tell their story. Zara Isa, Asma'u Adamu, Hafsatu (Gambo) Musa, Hassana Sa'idu, Maryam Musa, and Falmata Mohammed, your courage and openness will forever inspire me. I owe a deep debt of gratitude as well to Hauwa Umaru and Hajera Musa, Aisha Gombi and Aisha Wakil, the mother figures. And to Dr. Fatima Akilu, there are no words: we are all so lucky to know you. Thank you for being the light in the darkness.

Kabir Anwar, my collaborator, you took on so much when you agreed to work with me, and you deserve all the credit for this story. You have laboured tirelessly through your dogged reporting to ensure that the world doesn't forget about the victims of Boko Haram. Not to mention taking on the arduous task of fact-checking when the pandemic prevented me from travelling back to Nigeria.

Also in Nigeria, many thanks to David Otto, for being a fount of knowledge; to Charles Bob, for keeping us safe; and to

301

Peter Ebeh, Laraba Clement Yaga, and Aisha Bukar at Neem for the warm welcome.

To the team at HarperCollins Canada: Iris Tupholme and Noelle Zitzer, thank you for taking a chance on me the first time and never giving up on me since. To the best editor a writer could ask for, Jim Gifford, thank you for your patience and wisdom in guiding me through this process. This book was a long time in the writing. To my wonderful copy editor, Janice Weaver, thank you for your thoughtful notes and sharp eye. You have made me a better writer, and I will carry these lessons forward. I am so grateful.

To my guardian angel and manager, Perry Zimel, thank you for the gentle nudges when I couldn't write, and most importantly for the extraordinary gift of your friendship.

Some of you might be aware that this story was a documentary feature before it was a book, and I owe a great deal to the team at Antica Productions and TVO for believing in me and giving these girls a voice. Stuart Coxe at Antica, Linda Fong and Jane Jankovic at TVO, this is a testament to your vision and patience. Shelley Saywell, my dearest friend and co-pilot, your passion and clarity made me see what was possible, and your encouragement gave me the courage I lacked. I am so grateful for you and everything you've taught me. Brennan Leffler, my little brother, thank you for keeping me (and everyone else) on track in the field, for being my sober second thought, and for always being the first to be dragged into my crazy schemes.

To the film crew: Mark Klassen, Duraid Munajim, Brad Brough, and Peter Hamilton, you helped me see and hear things I would not have on my own. Your talents propelled this story.

Jon Wong, thank you for your vision. Seeing the film through your eyes put everything into focus. And to the brilliant Laurie Few, thank you for having the foresight to get this started all those years ago.

I am blessed with the most remarkable network of friends who kept me sane during the pandemic and without whose unwavering support I could not do what I do: Jennifer Burke, Denelle Balfour, Breege Walsh, Mason Clutter, Mark Walsh, John Noble, Heath Nash, Margaret Evans, Edith Champagne, Jennifer Barr, Kas Roussy, Angela Naus, Maureen Taylor, Kelly McClughan, Lisa LaFlamme, Rosa Hwang, Christine Nielsen, Stefani Langenegger, Coreen Moore, Julie Bristow, Wendy Crewson, Shelley Thue, Kiril Mumdjiev, Steve Chao, Craig Hansen, Jeanne Meserve, Christina Ford, Gillian Dobias, Ruth Rosenheim, Sarah Hacker, Seki Lindsey, Jeffrey Kofman, Michael Levine, Melda Bur, and Matt Cowan.

Thanks also to my family—my parents, Joyce and Kellog; and especially my sister, Vanessa, who makes me laugh and reminds me to take care of myself; and Pete, for keeping my glass full every time. To my brother and sister-in-law, Bob and Sharen Workman, thank you for always taking my side. And Caitlin Workman, for keeping me well dressed!

In the middle of writing this book, Afghanistan fell back under Taliban rule, and I had to stop writing; I was too distraught and distracted by the impossible task of trying to help at-risk Afghan women leave the country. Again, I was blessed to be connected with an amazing group of women doing the same thing, and they deserve mention here because I could not have got through this time and finished this book without their help with the evacuations. To Louise Penny, Allida Black, Megan Minnion, and Jane McElhone, what a source of strength and support you were (and continue to be) during a terrible time. Louise, you are a true treasure, and I am so blessed to be able to call you a friend. To everyone at Journalists for Human Rights, especially Rachel Pulfer, Jordan MacInnis, and Robina Aryubwal, who continue to work so hard to bring Afghans to safety. Don Dixon, thank you for taking over when I hit my wall. To Sharon Roobol and the team at Al Jazeera's premier documentary program, 101 East (especially Nick, Liz, Mav, and Andy), it goes without saying how grateful I am for everything you do (especially for keeping me employed!). And to Stephanie O'Keefe and her team at the International Women's Forum, your unwavering support has meant the world to me.

To Sandy Padwe, my first teacher, the one who instilled in me many years ago the values I still try to live as a journalist, thanks to you and Daphne for your continued love and encouragement.

And finally, to my first reader and editor and my North Star, Paul, who makes everything better and the impossible possible. I would not have been able to do this if not for you and everything you give me. You believe in me more than I do myself. I love you so much.

NOTES

1   Azeez Olaniyan, "Once Upon a Game Reserve: Sambisa and the Tragedy of a Forested Landscape," *Arcadia 2* (Spring 2018), http://www.environmentandsociety.org/arcadia/once-upon-game -reserve-sambisa-and-tragedy-forested-landscape.

2   "Why Boko Haram Took Over Sambisa Forest: Col A. Aminu (Rtd.)," *Daily Trust*, May 14, 2017, https://dailytrust.com/ why-boko-haram-took-over-sambisa-forest-col-a-aminu-rtd.

3   Abdulbasit Kassim and Michael Nwankpa, eds., *The Boko Haram Reader: From Nigerian Preachers to the Islamic State* (New York: Oxford University Press, 2018), 50.

4   Kassim and Nwankpa, 50.

5   Muhammad Yusuf, "Open Letter to the Nigerian Government," June 12, 2009: Muhammad Bakur, "waazin shekh muhannnad yusuf 1," YouTube video, February 17, 2011, https://www.youtube .com/watch?v=elVjD7znMik.

6   Kassim and Nwankpa, 179.

7   Kassim and Nwankpa, 181.

8   Kassim and Nwankpa, 195.

9   Alexander Thurston, "Chaos Is Worse Than Killing," chap. 3 in *Boko Haram: The History of an African Jihadist Movement* (Princeton, NJ: Princeton University Press, 2017).